P9-AOS-749

DATE DUE

MAR 14 1969

8 Jun '61
CITIZENSHIP
Jul 10 '61 C I T
Mar 6 '62 C I T
Aug 28 '62 C I T
Return to cit.
when done-

LC

8 Nov '63

CITIZENSHIP
18 Nov '63
Dec 17 '63 C I
Jan 7 '64 C
Mar 20 '64 C

CARREL
Oct '64

29 DEC '64 P K
27 MAY '65 P L
28 JUN '65 CS
6 JUN '66 IP
11 AUG '66 M K
16 SEP '66 M K
7 JUN '67 D
5 NOV '67 A K
1 7 DEC 1968 A

JAN 17 1995   JAN 17 1994

MANAGERIAL DECISION-MAKING

MANAGERIAL
DECISION-MAKING

A Logical Approach

R. W. MORELL, PH.D.

Chairman, Department of Business Administration
St. Joseph's College

THE BRUCE PUBLISHING COMPANY • MILWAUKEE

Library of Congress Catalog Card Number: 60–12650

© 1960 THE BRUCE PUBLISHING COMPANY
Made in the United States of America

658
M K 41 m

Ke 2 6 Fe 61
rec N₂ 16 063

To
MARION,
MARY,
AND
ANN

PREFACE

WITH the business scene becoming more and more complex in the era of automation, the time is now ripe for business to put its decision-making on a more rational basis. This present state of development calls for more knowledge on the part of executives, managers, and supervisors. For those who are already in management positions, the proposal that they make the relevant contributions of logical method a part of their personal equipment can be realized through various means. To begin with, independent study may be a suitable approach for some. For others, outside help may be necessary. Thus, evening management and supervisory development programs currently being offered by some universities, or company management development programs, or the counsel of a trained consultant could provide ample opportunity for managers and supervisors to gain an understanding of the relevant contributions of rational method to the recognition and solution of business problems.

Those still in school — the leaders of the future — should acquire the necessary background during their formal education. Otherwise, college students who enter industry may become somewhat disillusioned when they discover that they were never trained to solve problems and make decisions, activities in which they find themselves primarily engaged. Far too many errors in solving problems and in making decisions are due to loose reasoning and to an ignorance of the laws which govern the operations of the mind. We must think logically before we can act logically. College students would benefit immeasurably if they could be instructed in a system which they could apply "consciously" to their observations in practice. Such a system is the only effective way of developing the intellectual courage to face difficulties and to overcome illusions that are temporarily pleasant but ultimately destructive.

Accordingly, this book is intended for men and women: (1) who wish to understand better the process of making decisions; (2) who desire to improve the rationality of their decision-making; (3) who, like many supervisors, want to learn something about decision-making in order to teach others. The book is written primarily for use in an advanced undergraduate college course or a graduate course, including courses in business policy. Moreover, companies may find the book useful in their management development programs. At the same time, it may be useful in adult-education courses for businessmen. Finally, I have tried to keep in mind the needs of people who wish to learn something about decision-making by means of independent study at their leisure.

R. W. M.

Rensselaer, Indiana

CONTENTS

ix

x

CONTENTS

CHARTS AND TABLES

MANAGERIAL DECISION-MAKING

1 INTRODUCTION

THE business enterprise is one of the most important socio-economic units in the United States. Some 50 million people expect fair wages plus personal satisfactions and advantages from their jobs with roughly 4 million businesses; investors rely on these enterprises for the protection and conservation of their capital, as well as a return on their investment; and society expects these enterprises to provide the goods and services required by the needs and desires of its members.

Because management is of fundamental importance in assuring that businesses fulfill these obligations, it is evident that management is vital to both the individual firm and to the national economy. Although the functions of managers have been analyzed by numerous writers, a cursory examination of the literature will quickly reveal that there is no general agreement as to what the basic functions of managers are and what they should be called. In addition, practitioners and writers have tended to ignore one another in dealing with this subject. However, whatever else management writers and practitioners say that managers do, there is general agreement that one of the chief functions of a manager or administrator at any level in an organization is to make decisions. Although this may not have been true in the one-man companies of yesteryear, it is true today, and has been true for some time. Whatever the interest in the subject, the fact is that practicing executives, managers, and supervisors must be capable of making good decisions. This decisionmaking is the heart and core of administration; it is the key to business success and to the job of the manager.

1

In spite of its extraordinary significance, the subject of decision making has, until recently, received very little attention. Only during the past decade has the topic been discussed seriously in the literature and at conferences for management men — theoreticians and practitioners. If decision-making is the key to business success, it would seem that a great deal could be learned by analyzing the process and making managers conscious of it, especially where major decisions are involved. In this connection, executives are remarkably candid about their own ability to analyze the act of decision — usually they admit that they just don't know how they do it. Charles Cox, president of Kennecott Copper, says: "I don't think businessmen know how they make decisions. I know I don't." Benjamin Fairless, ex-chairman of United States Steel, asserts the following about decision-making: "You don't know how you do it; you just do it." Dwight Joyce, president of Glidden Company, states: "If a vice-president asks me how I was able to choose the right course, I have to say, I'm damned if I know."[1] William M. Day, president of Michigan Bell Telephone Company, in response to the query of the writer, "How do you make your decisions?" says: "I don't think we know how we make our decisions."[2] This very condition in which decision-making is so unfamiliar to skillful administrators detracts, unfortunately, from the confidence that can be placed in the decisions of managers — the leaders of industry. We can only mentally conceive the higher standard of living that would, perhaps, accrue to us if managers made better decisions which could result in greater efficiency, lower costs, increased quality, and reduced prices.

During the past two decades, we have seen important advances in organization theory and practice, in personnel management, in human relations, in management training, in economic analysis, in accounting methodology, and in mar-

---

[1] John McDonald, "How Businessmen Make Decisions," *Fortune*, LII, No. 2 (August, 1955), 85.

[2] At the Michigan Bell Telephone Company College Faculty Conference Meeting, April 2, 1958, Detroit, Michigan.

keting research. This understanding has resulted in significant improvements in our managerial competence. Over the next two or three decades the emphasis in management will be on the understanding of decision-making. This further understanding should be an even greater improvement in our managerial skill and performance.

Let me caution at once, however, against a rumor that is getting far too much circulation these days, namely, that business decision-making is going to become automatic in the future. Linear and mathematical (nonlinear) programing, quadratic equations, the theory of games, probability theory, search theory, operational observation, data derivation and deduction, statistical and mathematical theories, stochastic processes, matrix algebra, differential equations, symbolic logic, queueing theory, simulation, information theory, input-output analysis, and the like[3]—these are some of the esoteric terms for the new techniques in decision-making which some people would have you believe will take over, solve your problems, and make your decisions for you. Actually, some of these analytical tools, such as linear programing, probability theory, and simulation, are of proven value; others, such as quadratic programing, operational gaming, input-output analysis, and search theory, have potential value; still others, like formal game theory, appear to have little or no practical application. In general, these techniques are of greatest value where the effects of a large number of controlled variables must be considered, where the number of relevant uncontrollable variables is small, where relevant causes and effects are factual in nature and can be stated and measured symbolically or numerically, and where there are reasons to believe that past relationships will continue into the future. The main limitations of such methods are these: (1) factors of a value nature in decision-making must of necessity be excluded

---

[3] For a comprehensive discussion of these tools see Franklin A. Lindsay's *New Techniques for Management Decision-Making* (New York: McGraw-Hill Book Co., Inc., 1958).

because they cannot be described or measured objectively — one must temper his judgment with consideration of qualitative factors, even after all the quantitative tests are made; (2) specialists must work with assumptions that may not be valid, such as that personnel and capital will behave in the future as in the past; (3) mathematics and all its techniques cannot help in defining the problem; (4) it cannot make the decision concerning the best alternative; (5) it cannot implement the decision; (6) and, finally, electronic computers are frequently necessary because the utilization of some mathematical formulae would be seriously limited if economical computation were not available. Thus, until the intangible and unmeasurable elements that necessarily affect decision-making can be quantified, such techniques will have limited or no usefulness in certain areas of decision-making. Even the experts insist that the final decision can rest only with management,[4] and will continue to be made by human beings.

Accordingly, the manager who presently gets by without any knowledge of the decision-making process will tomorrow have to understand it and to use it. It is because of this vital need for study and analysis of the important management activity of "decision-making" that this inquiry is undertaken.

[4] "What's Ahead for Operations Research," *Business Week* (August 27, 1955), 64, 65.

2 THE NATURE OF DECISION-MAKING

FROM the beginning of the twentieth century when Frederick W. Taylor, the father of modern management, ushered in "scientific management," there has been a steady evolution of thought in the field of management. This "mental revolution" is becoming more and more significant in American industry. Tradition in management is being displaced by science in new areas and in new ways. Since science in management means the displacement of traditional methods by more rational methods, it is not surprising to find the "rule-of-thumb" managerial decision being subjected to some challenge. An intellectual break-through is shedding some light on the processes of decision-making. Experts in many areas of human activity are attempting to interpret the process in terms of their own specialties — logic, psychology, economics, philosophy, anthropology, sociology, operations research, physiology, communications, and many others. The researcher soon discovers, however, that it is difficult to mass these diverse contributions into a single frame of reference, often because his inquiries are unavoidably colored by his own personal preconceptions. A definition of terms, therefore, must precede any evaluation of any such contributions and of any conclusions to be drawn from them. "Decision," "judgment," and "decision-making" are the terms with which this study is concerned and which will now be examined in some detail.

DEFINITIONS

Decision. Various attempts have been made to define the term "decision." Etymologically, "to decide" means "to cut

5

off." In its present usage it suggests the coming to a conclusion. It "presupposes previous consideration of a matter causing doubt, wavering, debate, or controversy and implies the
arriving at a more or less logical conclusion that brings doubt,
debate, etc., to an end."[1]

A number of management scholars and practitioners, economists, and psychologists have also assumed the task of
defining "decision." Many writers have taken great pains to
distinguish "decision" from "habit" on a psychological basis.
George Katona, exemplifying the point of view of a psychologist, presents the following formulation:

> Genuine decisions . . . require the perception of a new situa-
> tion and the solution of the problem raised by it; they lead
> to responding to a situation in a new way. In contrast, habitual
> behavior is rather common. We do what we did before in a
> similar situation. . . . The main point is that the psychological
> process involved is different from that in genuine decision.
> Routine behavior, or using rules of thumb, are suitable terms
> to describe the second form of behavior.[2]

Chester I. Barnard, former president of the New Jersey Bell
Telephone Company, seems to sum up the findings of many
writers most succinctly:

> The acts of individuals may be distinguished in principle as
> those which are the result of deliberation, calculation, thought,
> and those which are unconscious, automatic, responsive, the
> results of internal or external conditions present or past. In
> general, whatever processes precede the first class of acts
> culminate in what may be termed "decision."[3]

Barnard appears to be classifying human behavior. His
statement may be interpreted as suggesting that human
behavior results from either conscious or unconscious
processes; and when these processes are conscious, they cul-

[1] *Webster's Dictionary of Synonyms*, 1st ed. (Springfield: G. & C. Merriam
Co., 1942), p. 224.
[2] By permission from George Katona, *Psychological Analysis of Economic
Behavior*, 1st ed. (New York: McGraw-Hill Book Co., Inc., 1951), p. 49.
[3] By permission from Chester I. Barnard, *The Functions of the Executive*
(Cambridge: Harvard University Press, 1938), p. 185.

minate in decision. The second, unconscious, or better auto-matic, class may well be called "habit." Most writers emphasize this distinction between conscious and unconscious action, the voluntary and the involuntary, although a few maintain that if the individual follows one course of action, there are other courses of action that he foregoes and thereby makes a "decision" even though it be merely a reflex action. For example, Herbert A. Simon takes this view:

> At any moment there are a multitude of alternative (physi-cally) possible actions, any one of which a given individual may undertake; by some process these numerous alternatives are narrowed down to that one which is in fact acted out. The words "choice" and "decision" will be used interchangeably . . . to refer to this process. Since these terms as ordinarily used carry connotations of self-conscious, deliberate, rational selection, it should be emphasized that as used here they in-clude any process of selection, regardless of whether the above elements are present to any degree.[4]

The term "decision" is used by Simon without any implica-tion of a necessary conscious or deliberate process. It refers simply to the fact that, if the individual follows one course of action, he thereby foregoes other courses of action. Indeed, Simon uses "decision" to refer to any selection process although it may consist simply in an established reflex action as, for example, when a typist strikes a particular key on a typewriter. Robert Tannenbaum defines decision as "a con-scious choice or selection from among a group of two or more behavior alternatives,"[5] while John G. Glover simply defines it as "the choice of alternatives, based on judgment."[6] George R. Terry calls decision "the selection of one behavior alterna-tive from among two or more possible alternatives."[7] Richard

---

[4] By permission from Herbert A. Simon, *Administrative Behavior* (New York: The Macmillan Co., 1947), p. 4.

[5] Robert Tannenbaum, "Managerial Decision-Making," *Journal of Business*, Vol. XXIII, No. 1 (January, 1950), p. 23.

[6] John G. Glover, *Business Operational Research and Reports* (New York: American Book Co., 1949), p. 12.

[7] George R. Terry, *Principles of Management* (Homewood: Richard D. Irwin, Inc., 1953), p. 106.

N. Owens writes: "A decision is the formation of an opinion or a conclusion, the termination of a controversy, or the making of a choice between possible courses of action or between persons."[8] Charles Jamison similarly states: "decision grows out of the choice of one course of action from alternative courses."[9]

A careful examination and comparison of the foregoing definitions indicates that there is a considerable amount of agreement among the writers. There appears to exist in their presentations, either expressed or implied, what may be called a keynote idea — the selection of one alternative from among two or more alternatives. This keynote idea leads to a number of implications.

1. If a decision is a selection of one from among several alternatives, then there must be a reason for anyone's making a selection. As everyone knows from personal experience, careful reflection on the appropriateness of alternatives is a burdensome task which requires mental effort and which should not be done aimlessly. It does not seem rational to reflect on the suitability of alternatives without knowing exactly why — the objective to be achieved. Moreover, without a goal or an end, there is no basis for determining whether or not a choice among alternatives is a sound decision. Thus, we may say that decision-making should be purposive behavior — guided by goals or objectives.
2. Since decision-making ought to be goal-oriented, a choice among alternatives is typically a choice among means to achieve some end.[10]
3. The selection or choice of one from among several alternatives implies a process of evaluation which culminates in a judgment. That is, reasons for and against one alternative and others have to be sought for and appraised. Ultimately, a final judgment must be made.

---

[8] Richard N. Owens, *Introduction to Business Policy* (Homewood: Richard D. Irwin, Inc., 1954), p. 115.

[9] Charles Jamison, *Business Policy* (New York: Prentice-Hall, Inc., 1953), p. 120.

[10] A small percentage of the decisions of an individual relates to his structure of values — these decisions determine his ultimate ends. Such value decisions are based upon the varying backgrounds and accumulated experiences of the individuals concerned. Since each person carries around a different

If these interpretations are accepted, the term "decision" must be provisionally taken to mean a judgment among ends or among means to achieve some end. But "judgment" is an ambiguous term; if it is to have value as an essential part of the definition of decision, the term "judgment" must in its turn be defined.

Judgment and Decision. Originally, a judgment was the action of a judge or magistrate who pronounced the right or law in a contested question — *jus dicere,* "to declare the law."[11] It has come to mean any action of the mind, which, after certain deliberation, pronounces the difference or agreement of two elements of thought. In the words of the psychologist Francis L. Harmon:

> Judgment is concerned with the conscious formulation of relationships among sense objects, images, or ideas. It implies apprehension of the things to be compared, as well as certain relational concepts of equality and inequality, and ideas of qualities like size, weight, goodness, and beauty. Mere perception of objects does not necessarily lead to expression of judgments regarding their interrelationships, nor does a sensorimotor reaction to some specific material relationship; for example, a difference in size, shape, or brightness, necessarily imply an intellectual judgment. . . . Furthermore, the understanding of a judicial statement does not constitute a judgment in itself. . . . Judgment, in a word, involves assent on the subject's part — an intellectual reaction, which, under some

conceptual structure or framework of ideas in his mind, decisions among ends are subjective decisions, that is, such decisions are measured by one's personal standards rather than by objective standards. All other decisions are directly or indirectly related to means. In terms of a means-ends hierarchy, intermediate goals are decisions made in the belief that they will serve as the means of achieving one or more ultimate goals. Since a decision among means is relevant to some goal, we have an objective basis (are the alternative means selected conducive to the achievement of the selected goals?) in this type of decision for determining whether or not a choice among means is a sound decision. In this connection, one very important function that an organization performs is to provide individuals with goals. To company goals an individual may attach his own framework of individual goals. With ends, goals, or objectives largely specified for him, the decisions of a manager are, for the most part, decisions among means.

11 H. G. Emery, K. G. Brewster, and C. H. Fitch (editors), *The New Century Dictionary,* Vol. I (New York: D. Appleton-Century Co., 1944), p. 883.

circumstances, may be either given or withheld. . . . Psychologically, an erroneous judgment is as genuine an intellectual phenomenon as a correct one; the difference lies in its validity.[12]

Andrew H. Bachhuber defines "judgment" simply as "the mental operation by which we affirm or deny anything whatsoever,"[13] while Celestine N. Bittle similarly writes: "A judgment is an act of the mind pronouncing the agreement or disagreement of ideas among themselves; or, in other words, it is an act of the intellect affirming or denying one idea of another."[14]

From these statements it appears that a judgment is an affirming or denying act of the mind. For our purposes, then, "judgment" may be taken to mean a definitively assertive intellectual act, that is, an act of the mind by which man positively affirms or denies something of something else. Such an act of the mind consists of three elements — the subject, the predicate, and the copula. The part of a judgment containing that which we affirm or deny is called the "predicate," the part containing that about which the assertion or denial is made is called the "subject," and the word or words which connects or associates the subject and predicate is called the "copula."[15] Thus, the "subject" has something said about it; the "predicate" is that which is said about the subject; and the "copula" expresses the act of the intellect in affirming or denying the predicate of the subject at the very moment of judgment.

Judgment, however, must not be confused with proposition.

---

[12] By permission from Francis L. Harmon, *Principles of Psychology*, rev. ed. (Milwaukee: The Bruce Publishing Co., 1951), pp. 358–359.

[13] This reference and all subsequent references from this source are by permission from Andrew H. Bachhuber, S.J., *Introduction to Logic* (New York: Appleton-Century-Crofts, Inc., 1957), p. 30.

[14] Celestine N. Bittle, *The Science of Correct Thinking* (Milwaukee: The Bruce Publishing Co., 1935), p. 90.

[15] These terms as used here have nothing to do with their meaning and use in English grammar. They are used here in the logical sense, not in the grammatic sense. See Morris R. Cohen and Ernest Nagel, *An Introduction to Logic and Scientific Method* (New York: Harcourt, Brace & Co., 1934), p. 30.

A judgment is a mental or intellectual act which is confined to the mind. The act of judging is a simple internal act of assent or nonassent; it essentially consists in the irreducible act of interior affirmation or negation. It is in the judgment that truth and falsity are found. The proposition, on the other hand, is the verbal expression of the judgment or interior act of the mind. For instance, an affirmative judgment is expressed in the following: Alternative *A* (subject) is (copula) the best course of action (predicate). A negative judgment is expressed in the sentence: Alternative *B* (subject) is not (copula) feasible (predicate). Propositions are formulated in sentences, but not every sentence expresses a judgment. Sentences which express a wish, a question, or an exclamation do not reflect judgments because they are not assertive statements.

Since a decision was provisionally taken to mean a judgment among ends, or among means to achieve some end or objective, and since a judgment is thought of as a definitively assertive intellectual act, the term "decision" may be formally defined, therefore, as an intellectual assertion (affirmative or negative) among alternative ends, or among alternative means to achieve some end.[16]

Decision-Making. At this point, it seems valid to conclude that since a decision is a judgment among alternative ends or among alternative means to achieve some end, and since a judgment is a definitively assertive intellectual act, decision-making is, therefore, an intellectual activity. This conclusion is not to be interpreted as meaning, of course, that all intellectual activity is decision-making, but rather that decision-making is one type or kind of intellectual activity.

---

[16] The terms "decision" and "choice" will be used synonymously in this discussion.

3 THE PATTERN OF DECISION-MAKING

DECISION-MAKING may be relatively simple in some instances; in other cases, however, it may call for the most demanding exercise of a man's judgment, reasoning, and imagination. In any event, a decision can be only as good as the process used to reach it. Accordingly, for those called upon to make important and difficult decisions, it will be helpful, if not essential, to be thoroughly grounded in the various steps of this process, to understand the theoretical and logical bases of decision-making. A businessman so grounded will be much better prepared for administrative work than one who makes decisions on a hit-or-miss basis or who simply has a few rules-of-thumb to go by. The purpose of this chapter is to provide a discussion of these theoretical and logical bases. This will help clear away some of the mystery commonly associated with the decision-making process, afford some insight into the nature of the process, and transform what is ordinarily an unconscious process into a conscious one. This is not to deny, however, that business managers, supervisors, and individuals may and do successfully make some valid decisions without any previous study of logical methodology. But it is also true that a person usually does a thing better if he knows what he is doing, why he is doing it, and how to do it. Thus, by securing an understanding of the decision-making process and by deliberately putting it to work for him, an individual should be able to augment whatever ability he may already have in this area.

Scientists, professional men, and laymen are all tied to logic. We can range only as far as our reason permits. The manipulation of the mathematical and chemical formulae of the scientist, and of the factual and value elements of the professional man and layman have little meaning unless they are dominated by rigorous logic.

Logical methodology enjoys a reputation that stretches back to Aristotle. Yet in spite of its great prestige, relatively few people seem to be able to reason logically, and even fewer seem disposed to accept decisions arrived at logically unless they happen to coincide with decisions previously reached on an emotional or volitional basis. Nevertheless, logic can give decisions-makers great leverage in solving business problems. Without it, the administrator and supervisor must put his faith in such untrustworthy methods as rule-of-thumb, impulse, or chance factors. Decision-making deals with problems and alternatives. Whether the decision-maker chooses one alternate or another depends very much upon his ability to reason validly. Mastery of logical analysis enables a decision-maker to get a firm hold on a difficult management problem or personal problem. Yet one does not need to be a master of the many technicalities to be able to understand and to use the principal processes of logic in the making of decisions. In other words, logicians have no monopoly on being logical. It should be noted, however, that it is not the task of logic to describe what happens organically and in the mind of the decision-maker as he attempts to discover and decide on solutions to problems. These are questions of psychology. Rather, it is the business of logic to guide the intellect with respect to consistency, validity, and order in the process of deriving a conclusion from one or more premises or antecedents.

Looking from the bottom of the managerial hierarchy upward, it may sometimes appear that decisions of managers and administrators are the arbitrary products of impulse and caprice. This should not be the case. A managerial decision should be based on premises or propositions. Sometimes these premises may not be precisely formulated, or may not be operative at the conscious level. But a correct and compelling decision is not a simple, unsupported assertion; rather, it is a conclusion which is sustained by the premises, or propositions, from which it is derived. The terms "premises" and "propositions" are used here in the logical senses, that is, as general laws, general truths, or principles and clear instances of such laws, truths or principles from which sound conclusions may be deduced. Thus a decision which is supported by the premises from which it is derived may be called a logical decision.

But this is to come in at the end of the play. The activity of decision-making does not begin with the formulation of premises. Earlier stages involve such considerations as uncertainty, analysis, consciousness of a problem, definition of the problem, formulation of alternatives, and so on. It is extremely important, therefore, that we begin our study with these beginnings, with the factors which initiate decision-making. For, as Northrop so aptly points out:

> One may have the most rigorous of methods during the later stages of investigation but if a false or superficial beginning has been made, rigor later on will never retrieve the situation.[1]

To begin with, let us consider the point at which uncertainty or doubt first swims into our ken.

THE STAGE OF UNCERTAINTY

Uncertainty or doubt is the first stage in the decision-making process. It is likely to be an anxious one for us, a period of worry and confusion. This stage of decision-making is aptly described by John Dewey as an "indeterminate situation," that is, a situation that is not settled, or, in other words, an uncertain situation. In fact, "it is of the very nature of the indeterminate situation which evokes inquiry [decision-making] to be *questionable* . . . to be uncertain, unsettled,

[1] This quotation and all subsequent quotations from this source are by permission from Filmer S. C. Northrop, *The Logic of the Sciences and the Humanities* (New York: The Macmillan Co., 1947), p. 1.

disturbed."[2] Nor are these characteristics of disturbance or uncertainty present in merely a subjective sense. "It is the *situation* that has these traits. *We* are doubtful because the situation [which is objective and external to us] is inherently doubtful."[3] This concept of uncertainty is a positive one. It does not mean a mere lack, absence, or deprivation in a purely negative sense, as would exist if the doubts were purely subjective states. Doubts which do not stem from a distinctive uncertain situation are "morbid" to the extent at least of being self-made and arbitrary. The uncertainty or doubt which sets the decision-making process in operation stems from a particular, uncertain, objective situation. The doubting which characterizes an uncertain situation exists because the constituent elements of a situation are not settled or unified. By an uncertain situation, then, is meant an un- settled or doubtful situation whose elements or factors do not hang together in a coherent or unified manner. It is Dewey's belief, therefore, that an uncertain situation, because of its "controlling presence," is capable of bringing decision- making into existence. As he states:

> The peculiar quality of what pervades the given materials, constituting them a situation, is not just uncertainty at large; it is a unique doubtfulness which makes that situation to be just and only the situation it is. It is this unique quality that not only invokes the particular inquiry engaged in, but that exercises control over its special procedures.[4]

To look at it another way, if Brand Blanshard were asked specifically about where decision-making begins, he would probably reply as follows:

> The immediate stimulus to reflection is always the appearance off the "mainland" of thought — the present accepted system — of an "island" — something which declines to be incorporated

---

[2] This reference and all subsequent quotations from this source are by permission from John Dewey, *Logic, The Theory of Inquiry* (New York: Henry Holt & Co., 1938), p. 105.
[3] *Ibid.*, pp. 105–106.
[4] *Ibid.*, p. 105.

— and the problem is always one of integration; how to bring these into an intelligible whole. . . . The movement of reflection starts when we are presented with something . . . which we need for any reason to fit into the system we carry about in our minds, and which yet resists inclusion. An island appears demanding union with the mainland; we must bridge the gap, but are at a loss how to do it; tension arises, and from that tension, reflection.[5]

The "mainland of thought," or the "present accepted system," as used by Blanshard refers to an individual's conceptual structure — the framework of ideas an individual already possesses. Every sane mind approaches an uncertain situation with a conceptual structure or framework into which to fit it.[6]

Then an "island" appears off the "mainland of thought." This is the stimulus which shocks the present framework or system of ideas into action. The gap between the "mainland of thought" and the "island" is actually a gap in an individual's conceptual structure brought about by the awareness of an uncertainty. The gap is so alien to the present conceptual framework that decision-making is initiated.

In short, then, we may say that an uncertain situation occurs when we find ourselves somewhat overwhelmed by a mass of seemingly contradictory facts that appear to need explanation and unification, or when we are facing a situation that is unpleasant or even frustrating and about which we feel we must do something but which we seem, to our dismay, to approach with a numb sterility of mind. For ex-

---

[5] This quotation and all subsequent quotations from this source are by permission from Brand Blanshard, *The Nature of Thought*, Vol. II (London: George Allen, Ltd., 1939), pp. 63–64.

[6] "But scholars and scientists come to a situation with an apperceiving system for a particular event that puts a world of difference between them and others" (Brand Blanshard, *op. cit.*, II, p. 77). In other words, the scientist and scholar (and this includes some administrators, managers, supervisors, and individuals), because their conceptual framework is being continuously built up through years of education and/or experience not only approach a problem with a well-constructed system of ideas which facilitates discovery and solution but also become much more sensitive to challenging problems while other individuals pass by undisturbed.

ample, the failure to achieve some business goal as evidenced by declining profits may impose itself upon us with a formidable array of revenue facts, cost facts, product facts, market facts, competition facts, organization facts, and so on. We become confused, worried, and vague; our mind seems to be a complete blank — a normal, but depressing, phenomenon during the stage of uncertainty. Or perhaps a supervisor is more than just casually concerned about the deterioration of the morale of his subordinates. Or an individual is troubled by the thought that he must soon replace his old automobile; or he may feel that something is wrong with his health because he seems to be tired all the time regardless of how much sleep he gets, how well he watches his diet and religiously takes his vitamins. If the decision-maker decides for any number of reasons such as time, cost, or effort that nothing should now be done about the uncertain situation, then, of course, the process is cut short and abandoned. But we are not interested in such negative behavior for the purpose of this analysis. Thus, an uncertain situation, as we shall approach it, is a disturbed situation which needs to be converted into a settled or resolved situation. The beginning of the transition from this uncertain situation to a resolved situation is commenced in the next stage of the decision-making process — the stage of analysis and definition.

THE STAGE OF ANALYSIS AND DEFINITION

"Uncertain situations" as discussed in the preceding section are not to be interpreted as being the same as "problematic situations." Although uncertainty is essential to the initiation of decision-making, more is required before we have a "problematic situation." The "uncertain situation," as Dewey stated, "becomes problematic in the very process of being subjected to inquiry."[7] This is a very important point. It means that analysis does not begin with the uncertain or unsettled situation — this is anticipatory to analysis

---

[7] *Op. cit.*, p. 105.

— but rather with the problematic situation, which makes explicit the problem implied in the uncertain situation. An uncertain situation becomes problematic when the decision-maker judges it to be such. This qualification is an initial step in stage two. When an uncertain situation is judged to be problematic, this very judgment not only acknowledges the existence of a problem but is also the first step in solving it. Since "a problem represents the partial transformation by inquiry of a problematic situation into a determinate situation,"[8] to render an uncertain situation problematic means, therefore, that what was originally doubtful is now partially settled because the process of establishing a problem has been initiated. Accordingly, a problematic situation is already on the road to settlement as a result of being subjected to preliminary analysis, whereas an uncertain situation is anterior to analysis and, consequently, is not partially settled.

Filmer S. C. Northrup, like Dewey, not only recognizes but also stresses the problematic situation. He believes that the decision-maker must begin his analysis with what he has at the beginning: namely, the situation which generates the problem. He therefore presents his own formulation:

> In the handling of any specific problem certain stages are to be noted . . . (1) the analysis of the problem which initiates inquiry, (2) the Baconian inductive observation of the relevant facts to which the analysis of the problem leads one, and (3) the designation of relevant hypotheses suggested by the relevant facts.[9]

Northrup places very great emphasis upon his stage (1) — the analysis of the problem. He believes this to be of primary importance because "all that one has in the beginning of inquiry is the problem which initiates it, and one must begin with what one has at the beginning."[10] Moreover, Northrup feels that analysis of the problem must precede all else because such an analysis guides the investigator to the facts needed to understand the problem clearly. "It is the analysis

[8] *Ibid.*, p. 107.   [9] Northrup, *op. cit.*, p. 29.   [10] *Ibid.*, p. 34.

of the problem which provides the criterion for selecting out of the infinite number of facts in the world the few that are relevant."[11] Thus, by analyzing the problem generated by the problematic situation, the decision-maker is led to the relevant factual situation — "the situation which contains the relevant facts to which the analysis of the problem leads one."[12] With the "problematic situation" reduced to the "relevant factual situation," the decision-maker is now ready for Northrup's second stage.

Stage (2) — the Baconian inductive observation of the relevant facts to which the analysis of the problems leads one — describes the relevant facts pointed out by the analysis of the problem in stage (1). "The important thing to note is that the second stage of inquiry begins with immediately apprehended fact and ends with described fact."[13] This goal is achieved through the Baconian inductive methods of observation, description, and classification. As Northrup expresses it:

> The second stage of inquiry comes to an end when the facts designated by the analysis of the problem in the first stage are immediately apprehended by observation, expressed in terms of concepts with carefully controlled denotative meanings by description, and systematized by classification.[14]

"Observed facts" are undescribed facts; they are perceived by observation but are not yet formulated. The moment they are conceptualized and are expressed in words, what was merely "observed facts," now becomes "described facts." The purpose of putting facts in described form is that they may take on the form of propositions or premises and, consequently, provide the type of material to which the methods of logic can be applied.

From the foregoing exposition it is clear that this stage of decision-making is analytical. More specifically, the analysis involved is largely factual; in it the decision-maker's first task is to separate the relevant, the material, and the significant

11 *Ibid.*   12 *Ibid.*, p. 31.   13 *Ibid.*, p. 35.   14 *Ibid.*

from the irrelevant, immaterial, and trivial. It is here that the decision-maker must discriminate between relevant and irrelevant fact, between assumption and opinion. In this connection, although facts are universal, it should be noted that interpretations of facts are personal. The decision-maker should be aware that his analysis of facts is dominated to a great extent by his conceptual framework. That is, the concepts and ideas that the decision-maker brings to the facts determine for him, if he is honest about it, what facts are relevant and significant, and what facts are irrelevant and, consequently, insignificant. A cardinal sin in this stage is, therefore, the manufacturing of facts. This takes place when the decision-maker has already prejudged a situation and wishes to build a case for his "decision of desire" by providing an illusory factual base.

The analysis of facts, which can be quite time-consuming depending upon the problematic situation, is only the first of the decision-maker's efforts in this stage. Another task, equally as difficult, is the definition or specification of the problem. The outcome of the analysis of the problematic situation which generates the problem should be a definition of the problem. The latter is the resolution of the problem into a question in order to render it definite and specific. This is achieved when the point to be settled has been made as definite as the case permits and has made explicit the facts and concepts already known which bear upon that point. As Blanshard writes:

> . . . the problem is specified . . . (a) when he [decision-maker] is clear what it is that he wishes to include in his system [conceptual structure], (b) when he [decision-maker] has assembled before him the set of data from which the solution must spring, and (c) when he [decision-maker] knows the . . . sort of connection, that, in accordance with the structure of the system [conceptual framework], would complete it satisfactorily.[15]

If the decision-maker is unable to state the problem specif-

---

[15] *Ibid.*, p. 74.

ically, preferably in one interrogative sentence which includes one or more goals, such as "How can the morale in Department B be improved?" or "How can the sales of Product C be increased?" then his analysis of the problematic situation has not been adequate or of sufficient depth. Therefore, further analysis is necessary. A word of caution may here be in order. Emotional bias, habitual or traditional behavior, or the tendency of the human being frequently to seek the road of least resistance may result in the decision-maker's performing a superficial analysis followed by a statement of the "apparent" problem instead of the "real" problem. An excellent solution to an apparent problem, of course, will not work in practice because it is the solution to a problem that does not exist. Consequently, a short-circuiting of the stage of analysis may actually result in more time being spent later to get at the real problem when the decision-maker returns for further analysis. The survival or continued success of a business enterprise frequently depends upon the ability of the decision-maker to see the real problem as it is projected in a dynamic business environment. A real problem well stated in one interrogative sentence is already on the road to solution. It acts as a directive indicating in which areas a solution should be sought. For example, if the problem is one of morale or sales as stated above, we already know that the solution must be one which solves a problem in the specific areas of morale or sales as the case may be. A solution would certainly not be sought in the areas of costs or production control unless the problem so indicated and directed. Alternatives and solutions are the subject of the next stage of decision-making — the proposal of alternatives.

THE PROPOSAL OF ALTERNATIVES

Once we have specified the problem, with what we believe to be a sufficiency of relevant facts before us, and with our previous knowledge as personal equipment, we may now formally[16] attempt the suggestion of relevant alternatives.[17] To Dewey this is a "progressive" matter. He states:

> A possible relevant solution is . . . suggested by the determination of factual conditions which are secured by observation. The possible solution presents itself, therefore, as an *idea,* just as the terms of the problem (which are facts) are instituted by observation. Ideas are anticipated consequences (forecasts) of what will happen when certain operations are executed under and with respect to observed conditions. Observation of facts and suggested meanings or ideas arise and develop in correspondence with each other. The more the facts of the case come to light in consequence of being subjected to observation, the clearer and more pertinent become the conceptions of the way the problem constituted by these facts is to be dealt with. On the other side, the clearer the idea, the more definite . . . become the operations of observation and of execution that must be performed in order to resolve the situation.[18]

It is clear, therefore, that the definite facts in a problematic situation must first be observed and allowed, together with the indeterminate uncertainties of the situation, to suggest ideas relevant to the possible solution of the problem. These ideas differ in grade according to the stage of reflection reached. At first, they are vague; but, as they function in directing further observation, the more suitable the ideas become in their capacity as a means of resolving the problem. As ideas become more appropriate, observation likewise becomes more acute. Perception and conception continue to work together until the former locates and describes the problem, while the latter represents a possible method of solution.

---

16 I say "formally" advisedly because we cannot dictate to our genius and, consequently, ideas may pop into our heads at any time or stage of the decision-making process without notice. Yet, if we have been a good drill-master in the past, it is amazing what we may deliberately create in the area of alternatives.

17 The terms "alternative," "hypothesis," "suggested solution," "tentative solution," "concept," and "idea" will be used synonymously in this discussion.

18 *Op. cit.,* p. 109.

Next the consequences of the suggested ideas or alternatives need to be developed. As Dewey wrote:

> . . . developing the meaning contents of ideas in their relations to one another . . . is reasoning. When a suggested meaning (idea) is immediately accepted, inquiry is cut short. Hence the conclusion reached is not grounded even if it happens to be correct. The check upon immediate acceptance is the examination of the meaning as a meaning. This examination consists in noting what the meaning in question implied in relation to other meanings in the system of which it is a member, the formulated relation constituting a proposition. If such and such a relation of meanings is accepted, then we are committed to such and such other relations of meanings because of their membership in the same system. Through a series of intermediate meanings, a meaning is finally reached which is more clearly relevant to the problem in hand than the originally suggested idea. It indicates operations which can be performed to test its applicability, whereas the original idea is usually too vague to determine crucial operations.[19]

The point to be appreciated here is the examination of suggested alternatives (ideas) with reference to their functional fitness, that is, the capacity of the suggested alternatives to operate as a *means* in the solution of a problem. This process involves examining suggested alternatives when stated in propositional form to determine their capacity to direct further observation in securing needed additional factual material. This examination may result in the rejection, acceptance, or modification of ideas in the attempt to arrive at more relevant alternatives. From such examinations into the meanings of ideas, the decision-maker is the better able to appraise the pertinency of the alternatives entertained.

Finally, the "operational" nature of facts and alternatives (concepts) — their capacity to interact or function together to bring about the resolution of a problematic situation — is Dewey's main theme. "The problem is insoluble save as it is recognized that both observed facts and entertained ideas are

---

[19] *Ibid., pp.* 111–112.

operational."[20] The operational character of facts and meanings has to do with the manner in which both facts given by observation and the suggested alternatives or ideas cooperate with each other to resolve the uncertain situation with which decision-making begins. Dewey stated that:

> Facts are evidential and are tests of an idea insofar as they are capable of being organized with one another. The organization can be achieved only as they interact with one another. . . . Some observed facts point to an idea that stands for a possible solution. This idea evokes more observations. Some of the newly observed facts link up with those previously observed and are such as to rule out other observed things with respect to their evidential function. The new order of facts suggests a modified idea (or hypothesis) which occasions new observations whose result again determines a new order of facts and so on until the existing order is both unified and complete. In the course of this serial process, the ideas that represent solutions are tested or "proved." . . .They [the facts of the case] are tested or "proved" with respect to their evidential function just as much as ideas (hypotheses) are tested with reference to their power to exercise the function of resolution.[21]

This significant interrelationship between facts and ideas — each conditioning the other — has already been mentioned above. However, one point does need further clarification — the testing nature of facts and ideas. Ideas are tested by their capacity to bring new facts to light and to organize the selected facts into a coherent whole. Facts are tested by their fitness to function as evidence. Both are finally checked by their capacity to work together to bring about a resolved situation.

Creating and figuring out alternatives and their consequences in connection with the problem and its characteristics and the relevant facts is thus a major part of all rational decision-making. Nevertheless, in spite of the prime importance of the use of alternatives in decision-making, "No

20 *Ibid.,* p. 112.
21 *Ibid.,* pp. 113–114.

rules can be stated for 'hitting upon' relevant hypotheses."[22] We do not know how the mind organizes, relates, and synthesizes facts and ideas. We do know, however, that after a period of prolonged, conscious study and analysis, a period of incubation sets in. Frequently, the decision-maker has ceased making a deliberate effort to solve the problem and has turned his attention to other activities such as recreation, relaxation, physical exercise, other mental work, or sleep. Time seems to be essential to the process as ideas reappear spontaneously from time to time with modifications permitting the decision-maker to cast and recast them, experimentally, in a number of alternative relationships. The length of time may last from a few minutes or hours to days, months, and even years depending upon the competence of the decision-maker, the nature of the original initiating situation, and the type of problem.

Yet there are several practices which a decision-maker can employ to increase the probability of formulating relevant alternatives. One is to realize that the alternatives are a function, in part at least, of the data and concepts at one's disposal. When these are sufficient, fruitful alternatives may emerge. Consequently, the decision-maker should be saturated in background knowledge of his problem. Another is to concentrate on the problem intensively for prolonged periods, preferably without anxiety and in a mood of eagerness, and then turn away from the problem and relax. It seems that tension and anxiety have a negative effect on the decision-maker's creative ability, whereas relaxation often seems to be the mother of hypothesis. In this connection the decision-maker might well carry with him a notebook so that he can quickly record the core of a good idea that occurs to him at what he believes to be a wholly inopportune time. Failure to do this often results in the loss of many of our best ideas because of our dependence on frail memory. In addition,

---

[22] Morris R. Cohen and Ernest Nagel, *An Introduction to Logic and Scientific Method* (New York: Harcourt, Brace & Co., 1934), p. 202.

when the decision-maker feels that he has reached a complete impasse, it is helpful to restructure the problem. Restructuring a problem involves manipulating the elements of which it is composed. For example, it may involve a change of point of view (looking at the problem as the other fellow sees it), or a permissible modification of objective, or a rearrangement of the other elements of a problem as it is stated. Such activities may stimulate alternatives not apparent in the original statement of the problem. Moreover, since the alternatives that a decision-maker can produce are a function of the totality of all the background and experience, facts, and concepts that he has accumulated up to the present time, he should take advantage of every opportunity to build up continuously his conceptual framework through education, experience, reading, study, and discussion. A well-organized conceptual system is analogous to a sword in the decision-maker's hand while he is at battle in the arena of choice. Finally, the act of creating alternatives will assuredly be more productive for the decision-maker who courageously and frequently attempts to solve more and more difficult problems over the years as the need arises.

THE STAGE OF VERIFICATION

The stage of verification is the final stage of the pattern of decision-making. This is the stage in which the decision-maker attempts to re-examine, to confirm, to substantiate, to test the alternatives developed in the preceding stage. It rests on the principle that a period of hesitation before adoption of any alternative to permit checking the alternatives is a characteristic of rational behavior. Most of us have many times experienced disappointment in realizing that an alternative which looked good initially is really quite impracticable upon verification.

There are informal methods of verifying alternatives, such as an imaginative projection of the possible effects if one or more alternatives were actually put into operation. However, this writer proposes the use of a more formal system of verification, namely, deduction. As will be subsequently demonstrated, logical deduction serves admirably as a check in the case of alternatives, holding up the logical conditions or standards that must be satisfied if an alternative is to be accepted as the final decision. To achieve the goal of testing our alternatives logically, it is necessary to state them in propositional form (verbal expressions of alternatives) in order to discover and test the implications of the alternatives and draw valid inferences from them. How this is to be done formally is the subject of the remainder of this book.

SUMMARY

The preceding analysis indicates that the pattern of decision-making includes the following four stages:

1. The Stage of Uncertainty;
2. The Stage of Analysis and Definition;
3. The Proposal of Alternatives;
4. The Stage of Verification.

Stage 1 — the stage of uncertainty — is a function of the state of development of a decision-maker's conceptual structure. A well-developed conceptual framework is sensitive to doubtful and uncertain situations. On the other hand, a less well-constructed system of ideas may fail to provide the necessary awareness of an unsettled situation and, subsequently, its accompanying problem. In stage 2 — the stage of analysis and definition — the decision-maker seeks to discover the relevant facts of the problematic situation and also to define and delimit the problem. The statement of the problem in stage 2, plus a sufficiency of relevant facts and the decision-maker's previous knowledge, may then be used to suggest relevant alternatives — stage 3. In stage 4 — the stage of verification — the logician, through his treatment of deduction, makes his cardinal contribution to decision-making.

Although the preceding pattern of decision-making appears in four neat stages, it would be misleading if the reader did not realize that the four stages may overlap in actual practice. Alternatives usually are not created by moving in an orderly sequence from the first to the fourth stage. It is not uncommon for a new alternative or idea to recur from time to time, while the decision-maker is still collecting data about the problem. Moreover, in a complex problem different phases of the subject may develop at different rates. For example, the decision-maker may have reached the verification stage for one aspect or subsidiary problem of a great problem, while still floundering around in the stage of analysis and definition on another aspect or subsidiary part of the major problem. Thus, in a complex, difficult problem, various stages may appear in different aspects of the same problem simultaneously. Nevertheless, it was necessary to approach the pattern of decision-making, stage by stage, in piecemeal fashion in order adequately to analyze the process and at the same time to uncover some meaningful and useful insights.

The practical use of this pattern of decision-making in actual decision-making situations will be demonstrated in detail in Chapter 9. Before this can be fruitfully pursued, however, it is necessary that something be said about the role of premises in decision-making, decision and implication, and that careful consideration be given to validating forms for decision-makers. Let us now turn, therefore, to the antecedents of decision — premises.

4 PREMISES—THE ANTECEDENTS OF DECISION

In the preceding chapter the stages of decision-making were examined at length. Stage 4 — the stage of verification — requires that suggested solutions or alternatives be stated in propositional form in order to discover their implications and draw inferences from them. The value of understanding premises[1] or propositions for the decision-maker lies, therefore in discovering what decisions may be validly drawn from them. Thus, as antecedents of decision, premises become basic raw materials in decision-making.

THE CONCEPT OF A PREMISE

Like logical analysis itself, the concept of premise or proposition goes all the way back to Aristotle. In the Aristotelian or traditional sense, a premise is a verbal statement in which something is affirmed or denied: it is an assertion. But not every sentence is a premise. Sentences which express a wish, a question, an exclamation, or a command are not premises because they do not assert an affirmation or a negation. In addition, premises or propositions are often confounded with the mental acts which they express. This confusion is fostered by using the terms "judgment" and "proposition" loosely. As already indicated in Chapter 2, a judgment is an intellectual act which is confined to the limits of the mind. A premise or proposition is the verbal expression of a judg-

---

[1] The term "premise" will be used in this discussion as found in *The New Century Dictionary:* "premise . . . An antecedent statement or proposition from which an inference or conclusion is drawn" (H. G. Emery, K. G. Brewster, and Charles H. Fitch [editors], *The New Century Dictionary*, Vol. II [New York: D. Appleton-Century Co., 1944], p. 883).

ment. In others words, a premise or proposition is the externalization of the judgment.

FUNDAMENTAL TYPES OF PREMISES

Categorical Premises. According to Aristotle, as noted above, a premise either asserts or negates something of something else. A premise which asserts an unqualified agreement or disagreement between two terms — the subject and the predicate — by means of a copula, which is always some part of the verb "to be," is called a categorical proposition or premise. Thus, like an unqualified judgment, a categorical premise, which is the expression of such a judgment, consists of three elements: (1) the subject; (2) the predicate; and (3) the copula. Moreover, all that was said about these three elements with respect to judgment as exemplified in Chapter 2 also applies to categorical premises, the expressions of such judgments.

Hypothetical Premises. Some premises, however, do not absolutely affirm or deny the predicate of the subject, but do so only conditionally or in case something else is true, while others present two or more alternatives, whereas others deny the simultaneous possibility of two or more alternatives. This class of propositions or premises is called hypothetical. Hypothetical premises are divided into conditional, disjunctive, and conjunctive premises. The conditional premise is composed of a subordinate clause called the antecedent and a principal clause called the consequent — this is the "If . . . then" type. For example, "If we lower the price, then sales volume will increase." The disjunctive premise is a hypothetical proposition which presents various alternatives and asserts that an indeterminate one of them is true. It is of the forms "Either *A* or *B*, but not both" or "Either *A* or *B*, maybe both."[2] For example, "Either a line and staff organi-

---

[2] Andrew H. Bachhuber, S.J., *An Introduction to Logic* (New York: Appleton-Century-Crofts, Inc., 1957), p. 159.

zation or a functional organization will be most efficient in this company." Finally, the conjunctive premise is a hypothetical premise which denies the simultaneous possibility of two or more alternatives. It is of the form "Not both A and B, maybe neither."[3] For example, "An executive is either indecisive or successful."

Factual Premises. As noted above, a managerial decision is derived from premises. While these premises are basically categorical and/or hypothetical, a decision may also be viewed as a conclusion reached from factual and/or value premises or propositions. This classification of premises is based upon the nature of their content rather than the nature of the assertion made, as was the case with categorical and hypothetical premises. A factual premise is one that is predominantly measured by objective standards, whereas a value premise is measured by personal or nonempirical standards. This means that a premise may be almost wholly factual or almost wholly value, or partly factual and partly value. A premise or a part of a premise which is measured by objective standards is one that can, in principle, be tested by some other means than one's personal standards, such as a generally agreed upon common denominator or measuring rod. For instance, if an executive in making some proposal suggested that the company would lose $10,000, each administrator present would visualize essentially the same thing — namely, that $10,000 of the company's resources would disappear if that alternative were to be pursued. The dollar as a measure is external and explicit, and it is generally accepted in this country as the unit of monetary value. It is objective and nobody questions it. Other examples of factual premises or factual parts or elements of premises include such items as units sold, units produced, units in the inventory; time; symbols used to refer to specific parts in the storeroom or machines in the plant; temperature; and so on.

Value Premises. A value premise or part of a value prem-

---

[3] *Ibid.*

ise, on the other hand, is one that is measured by one's own private measuring rod. All of us have gradually accumulated a battery of subjective measures out of our total experience. These are based upon the varying backgrounds and accumulated experiences of each individual. As a result, each person has a different conceptual structure by which he makes his value judgments. Thus, we frequently hear the statement "He made a value judgment" when someone does not agree with somebody else's opinion. Actually, in decision-making there is no escape from making value judgments because virtually every premise contains some degree of value characteristics. Moreover, even if we assume that we are dealing with purely factual premises in decision-making, it is continually necessary to choose premises whose truth or falsehood cannot be determined with certainty with the data and time available for reaching the decision. The serious difficulty with value measures, however, is that most of us tend to think of our own value standards as factual or objective; we frequently assume that everyone else universally uses the same value scale or value structure as we do. Actually, nobody has precisely the same scale of values however similar the total experience may be. Nevertheless, value premises are indispensable to the decision-maker because factual premises are often not available in anticipating favorable or unfavorable consequences of alternatives, or in dealing with imponderables, or in making decisions based upon inadequate factual information. Yet the decision-maker should be aware that he is using value premises and that they should be used with caution. The role of values and value premises in decision-making seems to the writer to be the heart of the problem of choice.[4]

THE TERMS OF A PREMISE

The word "term" is derived from the Latin *terminus* meaning both "boundary" and "terminal limit."[5] In logical

---

[4] See the appendix for an economic approach to the value problem.

[5] H. G. Emery, K. G. Brewster, and Charles H. Fitch (editors), *The New*

usage, a "term" is defined as "a word, or group of words, expressing a mental image,"[6] or "a sensible conventional sign, expressive of an idea."[7] Just as a proposition is the expression of a judgment, a term, likewise, is the expression of a concept or idea.

Because terms are the ultimate elements into which a premise can be resolved, a correct understanding of them is absolutely necessary if the decision-maker is to proceed logically from premises to decisions. This requires a consideration of the two basic aspects of terms.

Comprehension and Extension. Every term has comprehension and extension. Bachhuber defines the comprehension of a term as "the sum total of the intelligible elements of the quiddity [essence, or nature] signified by the term [concept]," and its extension as the inclusion of "the subjects signified by the term,"[8] that is, those subjects that it actually sets before the mind. Turner writes that "comprehension may be defined as 'the attributes, qualities, notes, or characteristics which the term implies, and which must be present in an object before the term can be applied to it,' " and "Extension may be defined as 'the individuals or groups of individuals included under the term and to which the term may be applied.' "[9] Cohen and Nagel have the following to say about these distinct, yet inseparable aspects of terms:

A term may be viewed in two ways, either as a class of objects (which may have only one member), or as a set of attributes or characteristics which determine the objects. The first phase or aspect is called the *denotation* or *extension* of the term,

Century Dictionary, Vol. II (New York: D. Appleton-Century Co., 1944), p. 1962.

6 William Turner, *Lessons in Logic* (Washington, D. C.: The Catholic Education Press, 1911), pp. 34–35. Turner defines "mental image" as follows: "A mental image is any representation of an object in the mind whether it be acquired by one external sense, or by several, or by the internal sense (imagination), or by a highly elaborate mental process (ideation), *op. cit.*, pp. 31–32.

7 Bittle, *op. cit.*, p. 64.

8 Bachhuber, *op. cit.*, pp. 17–19.

9 Turner, *op. cit.*, p. 43.

while the second is called the *connotation* or *intension* [comprehension].[10]

Thus, by the "comprehension" of a term is meant the sum total of the characteristics which determines its meaning — the reality which it designates. By the "extension" of a term is meant the sum total of the realities, whether individuals or groups, to which the term is applicable. These statements can be represented as follows:

Comprehension	Extension
Body	minerals, plants, animals, men
Body with life	plants, animals, men
Body with life and sensation	animals, men
Body with life and sensation and reason	men

The larger the comprehension of a term, the smaller its extension; and inversely, the larger its extension the smaller its comprehension. This is called the "law of inverse variation." Consequently, if the comprehension of a term is increased by the addition of attributes, its extension is automatically diminished. The utility of a clear conception of the comprehension and of the extension of terms will be presently demonstrated.

Interpretation of Premises. In the preceding section it was noted that the terms of a premise may be interpreted either in view of their comprehension or of their extension; that is, they may be understood to refer either to the attributes and qualities which they connote or to the individuals and groups of individuals which they denote. This brings up the question of how a premise shall be interpreted in order that it may be subjected to logical treatment. Actually, based upon the concepts of comprehension and extension, there are four possible ways of interpreting a proposition, as follows:

Subject	Predicate	Method
Extension	Comprehension	Possession
Extension	Extension	Inclusion
Comprehension	Comprehension	Concomitance
Comprehension	Extension	Indication

[10] Morris Cohen and Ernest Nagel, *An Introduction to Logic and Scientific Method* (New York: Harcourt, Brace & Co., 1939), p. 31.

Of the above four methods, logicians have generally adopted the "inclusion" method of interpreting premises. This method of interpreting propositions is, therefore, based on the "extension" of the subject and of the predicate terms of a premise, known as the "distribution of terms," which, incidentally, is the fundamental idea in the theory of the syllogism. Nevertheless, it must be emphasized that extension is a logical property that flows from comprehension. To interpret a term by its extension does not mean to abstract from its comprehension or to look upon it as a mere collection of individuals; it is, rather, to consider it as being something other than the multitude of individuals in which it is realized.[11] This something else is the essence (comprehension) which the term reveals to the mind — the nature realized in each one of the individuals denoted. Accordingly, the primary and essential importance of a term is its comprehension; extension is a property that presupposes and flows from comprehension.

When a term, subject or predicate, is used in its complete extension, it is said to be "distributed." When it is used in partial extension, that is, when reference is made to an indefinite part, but not all as in complete extension, of the individuals which it denotes, it is "undistributed." The practical problem is to determine the actual extension of the subject and predicate in premises. This involves determining the numerical or quantitative character of the terms as indicated by the number of entities specified by the terms.

Based upon the distribution of the subject term, known as the "quantity" of a proposition, and the positive or negative character of the copula, known as the "quality" of a proposition, the following four fundamental types of categorical propositions emerge: (1) Universal affirmative — when the subject term is used in its entire extension (distributed) and the copula is positive, the proposition is called "universal affirmative." (2) Universal negative — when the subject term

---

[11] Jacques Maritain, *Formal Logic* (New York: Sheed & Ward, 1946), pp. 22–28.

of a proposition is used in its total extension (distributed) and the copula is negative, the proposition is termed "universal negative." The subject taken in total extension makes it "universal," while the negative copula renders it "negative." Combined, these two characteristics result in the "universal negative" premise. (3) Particular affirmative — when the subject term of a proposition is used in partial extension (undistributed), that is, when the subject term signifies only a portion of the individuals constituting its extension, it is called a "particular" proposition. Adding a positive copula to a subject used in partial extension results in a "particular affirmative" premise. (4) Particular negative — when the subject term is used in partial extension (undistributed), and the statement is negative, the proposition is "particular negative." The subject taken in partial extension makes it "particular," while the negative copula renders it "negative." Combined, these two properties result in a "particular negative" premise.

The classification of categorical premises into the four basic types given above is the basis of the following forms of inference: opposition, eduction, and the categorical syllogism (a fundamental form of deduction). These forms of inference will be examined in detail in Chapters 6, 7, and 8. But, first, let us turn to an investigation of the important concept of logical implication; unless it is understood, it is impossible to appreciate and accurately comprehend inference.

5 DECISION AND IMPLICATION

IN THE preceding chapter it was pointed out that an understanding of premises or propositions is necessary for discovering what they imply in order that inferences or decisions may be validly drawn from them. But the implications of premises must not be confused with the inferences or decisions based upon the implications. The distinction of "inference" from, and its connection with, "implication" must, therefore, be carefully noted. The importance of this difference to the decision-maker becomes immediately apparent when it is realized that inferences or decisions depend upon implication for their validity. As Cohen and Nagel write:

> We *infer* one proposition [premise] from another validly only if there is an objective relation of *implication* between the first proposition and the second. Hence, it is essential to distinguish *inference,* which is a temporal process, from *implication,* which is an objective relation between propositions. An implication may hold even if we do not know how to infer one proposition from another. Thus an inference to be valid requires that there be an implication between propositions. On the other hand, the being of an implication does not depend upon the occurrence of the psychological process of inferring.[1]

Thus it appears that "inference" is the mental process of drawing decisions or conclusions from premises; whereas "implication," being a relation between premises or propo-

---

[1] Morris R. Cohen and Ernest Nagel, *An Introduction to Logic and Scientific Method* (New York: Harcourt, Brace, & Co., 1934), p. 78.

sitions as such, is not a psychological affair at all. The statement by Cohen and Nagel that "implication" is an "*objective* relation between propositions" precludes the possibility that implications are made by the decision-maker. He may make decisions, but he can only *discover* implications. The implications exist whether the decision-maker discovers them or not. Cohen and Nagel remark further on this very important distinction between logical implication and psychological acts:

The process of exploring the logical implications is . . . a form of research and discovery. It should be noted, however, that it is not the business of logic to describe what happens in one's mind as one discovers rigorous or determinate solutions to a problem. That is a factual question of psychology. Logic is revelant at every step only in determining whether what *seems* an implication between one proposition and another is indeed such . . . any investigation into the laws or ways in which we actually think belongs to the field of psychology. The logical distinction between valid and invalid inference does not refer to the way we think — the process going on in someone's mind. . . . Of course thought (and not mere sense perception) is necessary to apprehend such implications . . . our apprehension of the logical implication on which our inferences are based may be studied as a psychological event, but the relation directly apprehended is not itself a psychological event at all. It is a relation between the forms of propositions and indirectly one between the classes of possible objects asserted by them.[2]

The logically necessary connection between premises and decisions revealed in implication is not, therefore, a description of the way people actually think, but indicates rather what decisions may be validly inferred from other propositions whether or not they are, in fact, inferred by the decision-maker. The clue to the formal nature of implication is suggested by Cohen and Nagel in the final sentence of the immediately preceding quotation: "It [logical implication] is a relation between the forms of propositions and indirectly one between the classes of possible objects asserted by them." The

---

[2] *Ibid.*, pp. 13, 18, 19.

term "form" in this reference is the keynote idea. In this context, the term "form" means an "arrangement" of premises or propositions, and of the terms of premises or propositions according to certain logical properties to be discussed in subsequent chapters. Assuming premises are "logically related,"[3] the arrangement of the classes of possible objects asserted by the premises is what gives rise to the relation of implication. If premises or propositions are not logically related,[4] the relation of implication will not hold, because no assertion of implication is possible in virtue of the "form" or "structure" of the propositions, that is, by reason of the present arrangement of the propositions and of its terms. In other words, the "form" in this latter case is not a "validating form." An implication may thus hold for one arrangement of premises and of the terms of premises (a validating form) but not for another. Thus, the assertion that a decision is valid if it is based upon an implication means that the arrangement of the premises and its terms is such as to warrant the truth or falsity of the decision. Accordingly, logic, as a study

---

[3] Premises or propositions are "logically related" when the truth or falsity of one or more propositions limits the truth or falsity of other propositions (cf. Morris R. Cohen and Ernest Nagel, *op. cit.*, pp. 52, 56, 57). In this connection, the logical relation of implication does not depend on the truth of the premises or propositions offered as evidence. Cohen and Nagel state that, "It is a great error to suppose, as many have unthinkingly done, that in the reasoning we call scientific we proceed only from facts or propositions [premises] that are true. This view ignores the necessity for deduction from false hypotheses. In science as well as in practical choices, we are constantly confronted with alternative hypotheses which cannot all be true. . . . We generally decide between . . . conflicting propositions by deducing the consequences of each and ruling out as false that hypothesis which leads to false conclusions. If false hypotheses had not logical consequences we should not thus be able to test their falsity.

That a proposition has definite logical consequences even if it is false follows also from the fact that these logical consequences or implications are part of its meaning. And we must know the meaning of a proposition before we can tell whether it is true. But in all cases (whether a proposition is true or false) the test as to whether there is a logical implication between one proposition and another is the impossibility of the former being true and the latter being false" (*ibid.*, p. 9).

[4] Propositions are "logically unrelated" when the truth or falsity of one or more propositions does not limit the truth or falsity of other propositions (cf. Cohen and Nagel, *op. cit.*, pp. 52, 56, 57).

of the kinds of valid decisions based upon implication, enables the partial formalizing of the processes employed in successful decision-making. Let us now turn, therefore, to the logical properties of premises, an analysis of inference and the "validating forms" for decision-makers.

6 LOGICAL PROPERTIES OF PREMISES

THE logical properties of premises require a consideration of what is called "opposition" and "eduction." Eduction is concerned with the arrangement or transposition of terms within a premise, whereas opposition is concerned with the compatibility or incompatibility existing among logically related premises. Both eduction and opposition provide the means for making explicit the implication contained in a single premise (see conclusion on page 50).

OPPOSITION

The logical relation of opposition has been adequately defined by Bittle:

> The logical opposition of propositions is the relation which exists between propositions having the same subject and the same predicate, but differing in quality, or in quantity, or in both.[1]

Although any two or more premises having the same subject and predicate are logically related, they are not identical, but are characterized by variations. These variations are based upon differences in quality or in quantity, or in both.

Types of Opposition. An examination of the quantitative and qualitative differences in logically related propositions reveals the following four types of opposition: (1) Contrariety — if two "universal" propositions differ in quality, they are called contrary propositions and the type of opposition involved is known as "contrariety." (2) Subcontrariety — if two

---

[1] Celestine N. Bittle, *The Science of Correct Thinking* (Milwaukee: The Bruce Publishing Co., 1935), p. 126.

"particular" premises differ in quality, they are called sub-contrary premises and the type of opposition involved is designated as "subcontrariety." (3) Subalternation — if two propositions of the same quality differ in quantity, they are called subalternate propositions and the type of opposition involved is known as "subalternation." (4) Contradiction — if two premises differ in both quantity and quality, they are called contradictory propositions and the type of opposition involved is known as "contradiction."

Compatibility and Incompatibility. The problem of opposition consists in determining the compatibility or incompati-

THE SQUARE OF OPPOSITION*
(Designed by Aristotle)

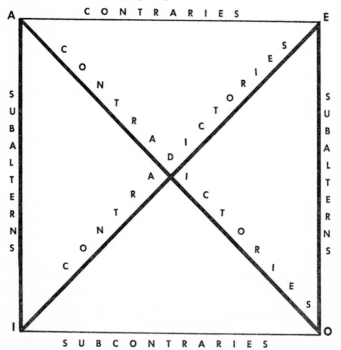

* SOURCE: Celestine N. Bittle, *The Science of Correct Thinking* (Milwaukee: The Bruce Publishing Co., 1935), p. 126.
NOTE: The four fundamental types of propositions are customarily designated as follows: *A* stands for universal affirmative, *E* for the universal negative, *I* for the particular affirmative, and *O* for the particular negative.

bility existing among logically related premises. If one of the propositions is given as true or false, the truth or falsity of the remaining three propositions is *implied* in the original proposition. The facts of consistency and inconsistency in the truth and falsity of logically related and opposed propositions are these: (1) Contrary propositions cannot be true simultaneously, but they may be false simultaneously. Furthermore, if one contrary proposition is supplied as true, the other is necessarily false; but if one is given as false, the other is unknown. That is, it is impossible to determine logically whether it is true or false. Thus, if either the *A* or *E* proposition is designated as true, its respective contrary *E* or *A* is inevitably false; but if either *A* or *E* is supplied as false, its respective contrary *E* or *A* is logically unknown. (2) Subcontrary propositions may be simultaneously true, but cannot be simultaneously false. In addition, if one subcontrary proposition is designated as false, the other is necessarily true; but if one is given as true, the other is logically indeterminate. Hence, if either the *I* or *O* premise is supplied as false, its respective subcontrary *O* or *I* is necessarily true; but if either *I* or *O* is designated as true, its respective subcontrary *O* or *I* is logically doubtful. (3) Subalternate premises involve the following facts. If the universal *A* or *E* is given as true, the particular *I* or *O* is inevitably true; and if the particular *I* or *O* is supplied as false, the universal *A* or *E* is necessarily false. But if the universal *A* or *E* is false, its subalternate *I* or *O* is logically unknown; and if the particular *I* or *O* is true, its subalternate *A* or *E* is logically indeterminate. (4) Contradictory propositions cannot be true or false simultaneously. If one is true, the other is necessarily false and inversely. Accordingly, if either an *A* or *E* premise is supplied as true, its respective contradictory *O* or *I* is necessarily false; or, if an *I* or *O* premise is given as false, its respective contradictory *E* or *A* is inevitably true.

Summarizing the results of the four types of opposition, the following list of valid oppositional inferences emerge:

Premises Given	Contradictory	Contrary
If A is true	O is false	E is false
If A is false	O is true	E is doubtful
If E is true	I is false	A is false
If E is false	I is true	A is doubtful
If I is true	E is false	
If I is false	E is true	
If O is true	A is false	
If O is false	A is true	

Premises Given	Subcontrary	Subalternate
If A is true		I is true
If A is false		I is doubtful
If E is true		O is true
If E is false		O is doubtful
If I is true	O is doubtful	A is doubtful
If I is false	O is true	A is false
If O is true	I is doubtful	E is doubtful
If O is false	I is true	E is false

To illustrate opposition, let us make use of the foregoing list of valid oppositional inferences. Take the following premise as given: Every manager is a decision-maker. This premise is of the A type — it is a universal affirmative. If it is true, then we immediately know, from opposition, that its contradictory O (Some managers are not decision-makers) is false. We also know that its contrary E (No manager is a decision-maker) is false. Moreover, we know that its subalternate I (Some managers are decision-makers) is true. If the premise "Every manager is a decision-maker" is false, then we know that its contradictory O (Some managers are not decision-makers) is true and that its contrary E (No manager is a decision-maker) and its subalternate I (Some managers are decision-makers) are doubtful, indeterminate, or in other words logically unknown. If, instead, we begin our reasoning process with the E premise "No manager is a decision-maker," and if we assume this premise to be true, where does it lead us? To start, we know that its contradictory I (Some managers are decision-makers) and its contrary A (Every manager is a decision-maker) are false. We also know that its subalternate *O* (Some managers are not decision-makers) is true. If, on the other hand, it is assumed that the original premise "No manager is a decision-maker" is false, then we know that its contradictory *I* (Some managers are decision-makers) is true and that its contrary *A* (Every manager is a decision-maker) and its subalternate *O* (Some managers are not decision-makers) are logically unknown. Third, if we commenced our reasoning process with the given true *I* premise "Some managers are decision-makers," what is implied? First, its contradictory *E* (No manager is a decision-maker) is false and its subcontrary *O* (Some managers are not decision-makers) and its subalternate *A* (Every manager is a decision-maker) are logically indeterminate. If, conversely, the premise "Some managers are decision-makers" is assumed to be false, then the following inferences emerge: its contradictory *E* (No manager is a decision-maker) and its subcontrary *O* (Some managers are not decision-makers) are true, while its subalternate *A* (Every manager is a decision-maker) is false. Finally, if the reasoning process begins with the following *O* premise (assumed true), "Some managers are not decision-makers," then we would know that its contradictory *A* (Every manager is a decision-maker) is false and that its subcontrary *I* (Some managers are decision-makers) and its subalternate *E* (No manager is a decision-maker) are logically doubtful. On the other hand, if the given premise "Some managers are not decision-makers" is assumed to be false, then its contradictory *A* (Every manager is a decision-maker) and its subcontrary *I* (Some managers are decision-makers) are true, whereas its subalternate *E* (No manager is a decision-maker) is false.

EDUCTION

Certain arrangements of terms within a premise are more effective than others in expressing equivalent truth or falsity. This accounts for the significance of changes in "position" in the methods of eduction called conversion, obversion, contraposition, obverted conversion, and inversion. In these methods of eduction the following rules are observed: (1) the same logical significance or meaning of the original proposition must be retained in the resulting proposition; (2) the distribution of any term in the resulting premise may not be greater than the distribution of that term in the original proposition.[2]

Conversion. The method of eduction which consists in transposing the subject and predicate terms without changing the quality of the premise is termed "conversion." There are two types of conversion: simple conversion and conversion by limitation (also called partial conversion).

"Simple conversion" consists in transposing the subject and predicate terms without changing the quantity or quality of the proposition. Hence, simple conversion includes three operations: (1) the subject of the original proposition becomes the predicate of the converse; (2) the predicate of the original proposition becomes the subject of the converse; and (3) the quantity and quality of the original premise remain unchanged. Since only in the E and I propositions do the subject and predicate terms have the same distribution, E and I alone can be converted by simple conversion.[3]

"Conversion by limitation" consists in transposing the subject and predicate terms of the proposition while changing their quantity but not their quality. Hence, conversion by limitation includes these operations: (1) the subject of the original premise becomes the predicate of the converse; (2) the predicate of the original proposition becomes the subject of the converse; (3) the quantity is changed from universal to particular or vice versa; and (4) the quality remains unchanged. Because the A proposition has a distributed subject term and an undistributed predicate term, it is converted by limitation.[4] "Since E propositions can be converted by simple

---

2 Bittle, *op. cit.*, pp. 136–141.

3 William Turner, *Lessons in Logic* (Washington, D. C.: The Catholic Education Press, 1911), p. 128.

4 *Ibid.*, p. 45.

conversion they can obviously also be converted by partial conversion [conversion by limitation]."[5] The O premise is not subject to either method of conversion, because in an attempted conversion the undistributed subject term of the O proposition would become the distributed predicate term of the result. This would violate rule (2) of eduction cited above (page 46).

Obversion.   Obversion is a form of eduction in which the quality, that is affirmative or negative character, of the proposition is changed, whereas the quantity, that is the universality or particularity of the proposition, remains the same. In obversion the subject of the original proposition is unaltered, but the predicate of the new proposition is the contradictory of the original predicate. This includes these operations: (1) a change of the quality of the original premise from affirmative to negative, or inversely; (2) the quantity of the obverse is the same as that of the original proposition; (3) the retention of the original subject term as the subject of the obverse; and (4) the substitution of the contradictory of the original predicate term as the predicate of the obverse. All four fundamental types of categorical propositions may be obverted.

Contraposition.   This is a process of eduction wherein the quality of the original proposition is changed, the subject term of the contrapositive is the contradictory of the original predicate, and the predicate term of the contrapositive is the original subject, while the quantity is or is not altered according to the type of proposition which is contraposited. Contraposition thus eventuates as the employment: first, of obversion and, second, of conversion. Contraposition includes: (1) a change of quality of the original proposition from affirmative to negative, or inversely; (2) no change of quantity in contrapositing A or O propositions, but a change of quantity in contrapositing the E proposition; (3) the subject term of the contrapositive is the contradictory of the original predicate;

---

5 *Ibid.*

and (4) the predicate term of the contrapositive is the subject term of the original proposition. The *A, O,* and *E* propositions can be contraposited; but the *I* proposition cannot be validly contraposited.

Obverted Conversion. In contraposition, "equivalent propositions" have been obtained by obverting and then converting. A different set of equivalent propositions are obtained, however, if the reverse procedure is followed, that is, first convert a given proposition, then obvert the result. This is called "obverted conversion."

Inversion. The "inverse" of a proposition may be effected by means of a series of obversions and conversions. The original premise is either first obverted or converted. Obversion or conversion are successively applied until the inverse of the original proposition is reached. Valid eductions are summarized in the Table of Eductions.

TABLE OF EDUCTIONS*

Original Propositions	A			E			I			O		
	S	a	P	S	e	P	S	i	P	S	o	P
1. Obverse	S	e	-P	S	a	-P	S	o	-P	S	i	-P
2. Converse	P	i	S	P	e	S	P	i	S	O has no		
3. Obverted converse	P	o	-S	P	a	-S	P	o	-S	O has no converse		
4. Contraposit, Type 1	-P	e	S	-P	i	S	I has no contraposit					
5. Contraposit, Type 2	-P	a	-S	-P	o	-S				-P	i	S
6. Inverse, Type 1	-S	o	P	-S	i	P				-P	o	-S
7. Inverse, Type 2	-S	i	-P	-S	o	-P	I and O have no inverse					

*Source: Andrew H. Bachhuber, S.J., *Introduction to Logic* (New York: Appleton-Century-Crofts, Inc., 1957), p. 70.
Note: The quality and quantity of each proposition is indicated by inserting *a, e, i,* or *o* between *S* and *P*. Contradictory terms are indicated by a minus sign (-). Obverted converse refers to equivalent propositions obtained by first converting a given proposition, and then obverting the result. Contraposit, Type 2, is obtained by obverting, then converting the obverse, and then obverting the converse of the obverse. Inverse, Type 1, is obtained by a series of obversions and conversions. Inverse, Type 2, is also obtained by a series of obversions and conversions, except here, you convert first.

The Table of Eductions can now be profitably used as the basis for a practical example of eduction. Since facts are so important to decision-making let us take the following four original premises:

A — Facts are universals.
E — Facts are not universals.
I — Some facts are universals.
O — Some facts are not universals.

Beginning with the A premise "Facts are universals," we can now determine equivalent premises by means of the quantitative relationships of terms and/or by the use or removal of negatives. Thus, the following equivalent premises may be derived from the original premise "Facts are universals":

Obverse:	Facts are not nonuniversals.
Converse:	Some universals are facts.
Obverted converse:	Some universals are not nonfacts.
Contraposit, Type 1:	No universals are not facts.
Contraposit, Type 2:	No universals are nonfacts.
Inverse, Type 1:	Some nonfacts are not universals.
Inverse, Type 2:	Some nonfacts are nonuniversals.

Similarly, from the premise "Facts are not universals," the following equivalent premises may be derived:

Obverse:	Facts are nonuniversals.
Converse:	Universals are not facts.
Obverted converse:	Universals are nonfacts.
Contraposit, Type 1:	Some nonuniversals are facts.
Contraposit, Type 2:	Some nonuniversals are not nonfacts.
Inverse, Type 1:	Some nonfacts are universals.
Inverse, Type 2:	Some nonfacts are not nonuniversals.

Again, from the premise "Some facts are universal," the following equivalent propositions may be educed:

Obverse:	Some facts are not nonuniversals.
Converse:	Some universals are facts.
Obverted converse:	Some universals are not nonfacts.

Finally, from the premise "Some facts are not universal," the following equivalent premises emerge:

Obverse: Some facts are nonuniversals.
Contraposit, Type 1:   Some nonuniversals are facts.
Contraposit, Type 2:   Some nonuniversals are not nonfacts.

CONCLUSION

The processes outlined in this chapter provide the means for making explicit the implications contained in a single proposition. Since the decision-maker is constantly dealing in propositions, he should be capable of handling propositions skillfully and accurately in order to analyze and test the premises of others as well as his own. In this connection, the decision-maker who masters the processes of eduction will not be required to "guess" whether one premise is, or is not, "equivalent" to another premise. Moreover, the transposition of terms within a proposition is useful to a decision-maker in the following ways: (1) to make explicit the truth which may be derived from any given proposition; (2) to discover whether or not any logical relations exist among a number of premises when the several premises relate to the same subject and predicate. Finally, a knowledge of opposition will enable the decision-maker to understand the relationships of premises to one another in regard to their truth and falsity — if one premise is false, certain other premises must be true, and conversely. Thus the decision-maker who possesses a knowledge of opposition will be able to make valid judgments concerning the compatibility or incompatibility existing among logically related propositions. It will be no mystery to him that between two contradictories there is no compatibility, whereas in the cases of two contraries, two subcontraries, and two subalternates, there is this much compatibility that they may be either false, true, or true and false respectively.

7 INDUCTION AND DECISION-MAKING

As USEFUL as opposition and eduction are to a decision-maker, they have their limitations. Opposition and eduction do not lead the mind very far because they merely make explicit what is implicitly contained in a given premise. The superior mental operation of a decision-maker is inference — induction and deduction — in which the decision-maker passes from premises to a conclusion. Since decision-making has already been described as an intellectual activity, it is obvious that the effective decision-maker should also be a skilled logician. Yet, few persons are conscious of the process of reasoning they employ to reach their everyday decisions. The administrator and the supervisor, however, are professional logicians; they get paid for deciding well. It does not seem unreasonable to the writer, then, that managers should be familiar with the most useful tools of their profession. Let us take a further look at more of these tools.

INTRODUCTION

Although most logical processes engaged in by the average man mingle inductive and deductive methods inextricably, the two are clearly distinguishable, and they are the major forms of reasoning. As the word "induction" itself indicates, to reason inductively is to be led, as it were, from one position to another until a decision is reached. Induction, then, is the process of reasoning or inference in which the decision-maker reasons from individual instances to a general conclusion. It is the observation of a series of phenomena until a pattern begins to emerge, at which point a provisional generalization is formed. It is the logic underlying all attempts to solve problems empirically, that is, by experience and by experiment. Employed conscientiously, the inductive method avoids prejudice and preconceptions, since the honest decision-maker will not devise explanations until the data support them and he will revise his generalizations when the discovery of new evidence requires it.

TYPES OF INDUCTION

Enumerative Induction. The inferring of a generalization from the accumulation or enumeration of instances is called enumerative induction. Two kinds of enumerative induction may be distinguished: incomplete and complete. When the induction is based upon a limited number of instances, the process is called incomplete induction. Such an induction can give only probability, not certitude. The probability of the inference may be increased, however, by additional evidence as the enumeration approaches completeness. Statistical method, which is a method of dealing with instances or observations, is an example of incomplete induction. When statistics on employment, unemployment, labor turnover, industrial accidents, investment yields, working capital, inventory, cancer, accidental automobile deaths, or any other phenomenon are cited, instances are being employed. One unemployed person is one instance. One half million unemployed reported in a given area are one half million instances. An inference from such statistics or instances is reasoning by incomplete enumerative induction. Thus, when we speak generally of induction without qualification, incomplete induction is what we usually have in mind.

On the other hand, sometimes we take particular instances and enumerate them *completely*. We then infer a general statement regarding the whole class or genus to which they belong. Thus, we observe that steel, copper, aluminum, silver, and so on, conduct heat. We conclude, therefore, that all metal conducts heat. It now makes sense to us why cooking utensils are made of metal, why the exteriors of homes are usually brick or wood (not metal), and why metal chairs are hot and uncomfortable to sit in during the summer months.

Scientific Induction. Two types of scientific or causal induction may be distinguished: intellective (abstractive) and rational. "Intellective induction . . . is the process whereby our minds rise from a consideration of particular cases to a universal truth because we understand *through insight into the particular case* that the universal is necessarily true," whereas "Rational induction . . . is the process whereby our minds rise from a consideration of particular cases to a universal judgment because we know, or at least have reason to think, that the judgment is necessary, although we do not see the reason for this necessity."[1] Both incomplete and complete enumerative induction may be either intellective or rational. Thus, these two divisions are not mutually exclusive — that is, they overlap each other.

Intellective induction, abstractive induction, or induction by insight, as it is sometimes called, is the ideal type of scientific induction because it depends upon no previous judgments and gives absolute certainty. Moreover, in abstractive induction, the decision-maker sees and understands the intrinsic necessity and, therefore, the full intelligibility of the universal judgment inferred from the particular instances. For example, in observing an organization chart of a business firm or a hospital, or a piece of pie, or an automobile, we know by insight that in each of these cases the whole is greater than any of its parts. In such an inference, the generalization is implicit in the knowledge of each single instance. The citing of the three instances above was done only for illustrative purposes. Any one of them would adequately support the generalization that a whole is greater than its parts.

Abstractive induction is the most fundamental operation of the mind, for all knowledge is ultimately inductive in origin.

---

[1] Andrew H. Bachhuber, S.J., *An Introduction to Logic* (New York: Appleton-Century-Crofts, 1956), pp. 299, 301.

Not all knowledge can be gained through previous knowledge. The premises of a valid argument may, it is true, be conclusions drawn from prior premises. But ultimately there must be direct immediate knowledge as the basis for all further knowledge. And this direct, immediate knowledge, whereby we gain insight into the natures or essences of things, is the knowledge given in abstractive induction.[2]

On the other hand, rational induction, a less perfect type of scientific induction, rests upon previous judgments and by itself only gives probability. In addition, rational induction relies upon a multiplicity of instances as evidence to support the generalization. Thus, if based upon a series of observations or a few carefully conducted experiments, the decision-maker discovers that A is the cause of E (effect), he may be warranted in saying that all A is the cause of all E (effect). Such conclusions are based upon previous judgments as the principle of the uniformity of nature (like causes produce like effects), and the principle of causality (every effect has a cause).[3] The establishment of a cause by means of rational induction based upon observation, experiment, and the like may ultimately lead to a stage in which intelligibility itself is displayed in the affirmation of the causal relation so that the relationship no longer depends upon the previous rational induction because it is now self-evident by insight (intellective induction).

RELATION OF INDUCTION AND DEDUCTION

Unlike induction, which proceeds from individual instances to a universal truth, deduction proceeds from the general to the particular. Deductive reasoning begins with general truths, general laws, or principles, and applies them to individual situations. It is the method best illustrated by mathematics.

---

[2] Vincent E. Smith, *The Elements of Logic* (Milwaukee: The Bruce Publishing Company, 1956), pp. 158–161.

[3] These principles are frequently referred to as self-evident truths because they cannot and need not be proved; they need only be explained to show their truth and validity.

The heart of the process is the syllogism, with its well-known major and minor premises, and conclusion. In deduction, the decision or conclusion is an explicit expression of the implicit relationship contained in the major and minor premises. It is an operation whereby the mind arrives at a decision from a set of logically related premises or propositions.

Although the trends of induction and deduction are in opposite directions, an intimate relation exists between them. Reasoning about problems combines building up generalizations from instances (data) and applying generalizations to instances in kaleidoscopic mixture. To make logic work in decision-making, it is necessary to keep a sharp eye on this blending of induction and deduction; the combination is inevitable in the solution of most difficult problems. In this connection Cohen and Nagel state:

> . . . deduction is not concerned with the truth or falsity of its premises, while the characteristic nature of induction is to be concerned with just that. Induction may therefore be viewed as the method by means of which the material truth of the premises is established.[4]

Induction, accordingly, furnishes the factual material and generalizations which may then serve as premises for deduction. It is precisely because induction provides the "material truth" of premises that it has not the "validating forms" that govern deduction. Induction is not reducible to "logical forms" that are valid regardless of their truth or falsity, but depends for its validity on the special character or material content of the data under consideration. Hence, there are no validating forms or rules for making the "inductive ascent" from the particular instances to the more universal.

DIRECTIVES FOR INDUCTIVE METHOD

Although there are no rules governing induction such as the rules for deduction which will be given in the next

---

[4] Morris R. Cohen and Ernest Nagel, *An Introduction to Logic and Scientific Method* (New York: Harcourt, Brace & Co., 1934), p. 278.

chapter, directives on how to conduct a search for order among facts in a problematic situation to facilitate the "inductive ascent" have been suggested. Cohen and Nagel assert that:

> . . . an analysis of the situation [problematic] must be made into a certain number of factors, present or absent, which are believed to be relevant to the solution of the problem. Now the order among the facts for which we are in search is expressible . . . in the form: C [cause] is invariably connected with E [effect]. And this means that no factor can be regarded as a cause if it is present while the effect is absent, or if it is absent while the effect is present, or if it varies in some manner while the effect does not vary in some corresponding manner.[5]

John Stuart Mill[6] gave a more explicit expression to this "invariable connection" between cause and effect in his "experimental methods." He summarized his teaching in five methods or "canons" of induction: The Method of Agreement: "If two or more instances of the phenomenon under investigation have only one circumstance in common, the circumstance in which alone all the instances agree, is the cause (or effect) of the given phenomenon." The Method of Difference: "If an instance in which the phenomenon under investigation occurs, and an instance in which it does not occur, have any circumstance in common save one, that one occurring only in the former; the circumstance in which the two instances differ, is the effect, or cause, or a necessary part of the cause, of the phenomenon." The Joint Method of Agreement and Difference: "If two or more instances in which the phenomenon occurs have only one circumstance in common, while two or more instances in which it does not occur have nothing in common save the absence of that circumstance; the circumstance in which alone the two sets of instances differ, is the effect, or cause, or a necessary part of the cause, of the phenomenon." The Method of Concomitant Variation: "Whatever phenomena varies in any manner

---

[5] *Ibid.*, p. 250.

[6] John Stuart Mill, *A System of Logic* (London: Harrison & Co., 1843), II, Chap. VIII.

whenever another phenomenon varies in some particular manner, is either a cause or an effect of that phenomenon, or is connected with it through some fact of causation." The Method of Residues: "Subduct from any phenomenon such part as is known by previous inductions to be the effect of certain antecedents, and the residue of the phenomenon is the effect of the remaining antecedents."

Although these methods, or principles, like most basic principles, are distillations of common sense, Mill claimed too much for them. Mill not only believed that the use of his canons could discover the order in which facts stand to one another, but he also maintained that *all* inferences are made by means of them. Moreover, he believed that his methods had a demonstrative or proof function; it was claimed that an induction was valid and absolutely certain if it conformed to the "experimental methods." For such high claims Mill has been severely criticized by many logicians. For example, the imperfection of the Method of Agreement is that a phenomenon may have several causes. Also, the Method of Difference cannot guarantee with certainty that the sufficient conditions for a phenomenon have been found because the factor noted may be only a "necessary part" of the cause. Moreover, the Joint Method of Agreement and Difference simply combines the limitations of the first two methods. In addition, the Method of Concomitant Variation can be employed only if degrees or magnitudes of effects and causes can be distinguished. Finally, since the Method of Residues derives its conclusions from inductions (premises) already established, this method actually operates as a deductive process. But, while Mill's methods do have the defects pointed out, they are nevertheless of undoubted value in eliminating irrelevant facts in the process of attaining truth in the inductive stage of decision-making: Stage Two — the stage of analysis and definition.

8 DEDUCTION AND DECISION-MAKING

In deduction, unlike induction, "validating forms and rules" have been developed to assist the decision-maker in drawing a valid decision from logically related premises. The validating forms and rules governing deduction are those of the syllogism, the syllogism being the typical form of deductive reasoning. Since the syllogism is the heart of the deductive process, it is important to understand its nature and structure.

THE SYLLOGISM

The syllogism is that form of reasoning or inference which derives from two given premises a third proposition, a conclusion or decision whose validity follows from the two premises as a necessary consequence. A syllogism, therefore, consists of three propositions. All the principles and rules of the syllogism are designed to show how propositions can be combined to yield valid conclusions by a process of reasoned interpretation. Syllogistic reasoning must begin with certain given premises in an attempt to see what they mean and to what they lead. As noted in Chapter 7, deduction, and consequently the syllogism, are not concerned with the material truth or falsity of the premises (this is the role of induction) with which it deals, but rather with the *formal truth* or *validity* of the decisions made from these premises.[1] It can be said of a *valid* syllogism that, if the premises are true, then the decision also is true and valid. If the premises are false, then the decision is valid (from a logical point of view) but false. Thus, deductive logic does not concern itself in any way

---

[1] On this point, however, note the remarks that will be given in our discussion of the middle term on p. 60.

about the truth of the premises, but only about the *cogency* of the argument. This consists in showing that the conclusion follows as a necessary consequence of the relationship which exists between the premises. Indeed, the conclusion is no more than the expression of that relationship. Consequently, the "form" of the syllogism is the nexus between the two premises and the conclusion. It is the sequence, the conclusive force, the convincing power, that binds the conclusion to the premises. The "form" is the very essence of the syllogism, its strength and cogency. It follows, then, that, if the reasoning mind admits the premises, it must likewise admit the conclusion.

Types of Syllogisms. The two fundamental types of syllogisms ordinarily distinguished are the categorical and the hypothetical. The categorical syllogism is one which consists entirely of categorical propositions as defined in Chapter 4. Every categorical syllogism consists of three propositions which serve to relate three *terms,* a major term, a minor term, and a middle term. Each of these terms is thought of as constituting a *class* (the sum total of the realities, either individuals or groups, to which the term is applicable) and it is the relation of these classes with respect to *inclusion,* one with another, which comprises the inferential process of the categorical syllogism. An understanding of these component elements of a categorical syllogism may begin with an analysis of the decision, or third proposition. The subject of the conclusion, or third proposition, is called the "minor term," and the predicate of the conclusion is called the "major term," and that term which appears in the first two propositions but not in the third proposition is called the "middle term." The proposition which contains the minor term is known as the "minor premise," and the proposition which contains the major term is called the "major premise." The categorical syllogism is essentially a process of *comparison* in which the minor and the major terms are compared with the middle term. In the major premise, the major term is compared with the middle term, and in the minor premise, the minor term is compared with the middle term. This operation allows one to compare the relationship discovered in the major premise with the relationship found in the minor premise. For example, if $B = C$ and $A = B$, then $A = C$. In this case $B = C$ is the major premise with C as the major term; $A = B$ is the minor premise with A as the minor term; the middle term B appears in both the major and minor premises but not in the conclusion $A = C$. The subsequent recognition and pronouncement of a new relationship in the comparison of the major and minor terms with the middle term is a "mediated judgment," constituting the decision. This act is a judgment because it is an assertion of the relationship discovered between the minor and major terms; and it is a *mediated* judgment because this relationship is not discovered directly by an immediate comparison of the minor and major terms, but by a comparison of them with the common middle term.

The middle term is the basic key to the construction of valid syllogisms. It represents the cause or reason why the minor and major terms are or are not united.

Here we should also note that the nature of the middle term gives us one means of testing the truth or falsity of a syllogism, and it thus saves the logic of syllogism from being something merely formed. The reason for this is that middle terms can be examined to discover their certainty, probability, or hypothetical character. If the middle term expresses the precise reason why the minor and major terms must be united, then the syllogism will give certain and true knowledge. If the middle term does *not* express this reason, but rather a plausible or persuasive basis for joining the major and minor terms, then the conclusion will have hypothetical or merely persuasive value.

Unlike the categorical syllogism, which is composed solely of categorical propositions, the hypothetical syllogism must possess at least one hypothetical proposition (as defined in

Chapter 4) as one of its premises, in which case the remaining propositions are categorical. Since a hypothetical syllogism must contain at least one hypothetical proposition as one of its premises, it follows that there will be as many types of hypothetical syllogisms as there are types of hypothetical propositions, namely, three: the conditional, the disjunctive, and the conjunctive.

The conditional syllogism, the most important among the hypothetical syllogisms, is that form of syllogistic reasoning in which the major premise is a conditional proposition composed of a subordinate clause called the antecedent, and a principal clause called the consequent, while the minor premise and the conclusion are categorical propositions. The validity of this type of reasoning process is dependent upon the relation existing between the antecedent and the consequent in the major premise. In a conditional syllogism the minor premise must either affirm the antecedent or deny the consequent. That is, if the minor premise affirms the antecedent of the conditional major premise, then the conclusion must affirm the consequent; and, if the minor premise denies the consequent of the conditional major premise, the conclusion must deny the antecedent.

In the disjunctive syllogism the major premise is a disjunctive proposition which presents various alternatives and asserts that an indeterminate one of them is true, while the minor premise and the conclusion are categorical propositions. The major premise sets forth two or more alternatives and the minor premise makes a selection among these by affirmation or negation. If the categorical minor premise affirms one or more of the alternatives of the disjunctive major premise, the categorical conclusion denies the remaining alternatives. If, on the other hand, the categorical minor premise denies one or more of the alternatives of the disjunctive major premise, the categorical conclusion affirms the remaining alternatives (see chart on p. 69).

In the conjunctive syllogism, the one which presents the

least difficulty among the hypothetical syllogisms, the major premise is a conjunctive proposition which denies the simultaneous possibility of two or more alternatives, while the minor premise and the conclusion are categorical propositions. If the minor premise asserts one member of the conjunctive major premise, the conclusion must deny the other or others (see chart on p. 69).

Rules of the Categorical Syllogism. The rules or axioms of the syllogism are both general and special. These rules are not arbitrary, but are based on the nature of valid syllogistic inference. These rules state the conditions which are necessary for the achievement of a valid deductive reasoning process. They are statements of what must and what must not be done in constructing the syllogism. Accordingly, the syllogistic rules simply declare how and under what conditions propositions must be combined to form antecedents which will yield a valid decision.

A categorical syllogism is not valid if it violates any of the following rules: (1) it must contain three and only three terms. The most common violation of this rule is to use a term having more than one meaning, giving it one meaning in one premise and another in another premise. (2) No term may have a wider extension in the conclusion than it had in the premises. Terms may have less extension in the conclusion than in the premises, or equal extension, but not more. (3) The middle term must be distributed at least once. This means that the middle term must be used at least once with universal extension. (4) From two negative premises, no conclusion can be drawn. The reason why this is true is that, if both premises are negative, the major and minor terms are seen to *differ* from the middle term, but we have no idea of their positive relationship to each other. (5) The conclusion must follow the weaker part. By "weaker part" is meant negative and particular propositions in comparison to affirmative and universal propositions. Hence, if one of the premises is negative, the conclusion will be negative; if one of the premises is particular, the conclusion must be particular. Some logicians also add another rule, which states that no conclusion follows from two particular premises. But this rule is really another way of stating Rule 3, for if the middle term is distributed at least once, then one of the premises at least must be universal.[2]

Rules of the Hypothetical Syllogism. With respect to the hypothetical syllogism, there are special rules governing the different kinds of hypothetical syllogism. The rules of the conditional syllogism are direct applications of the laws[3] governing the relationship of an antecedent and its consequent. The concept of *sequence* is especially important in this relationship. As Bachhuber writes:

> The assent in a conditional proposition does not bear on either the antecedent of the consequent taken by itself, but on the connection between them — that is, on the *sequence*. Thus, if the truth of the consequent really follows upon the fulfillment of the condition stated in the antecedent, the proposition is true even if, taken singly, both the antecedent and the consequent are false. And if the truth of the consequent does not follow upon the fulfillment of the condition stated in the antecedent, the proposition is false even if, taken singly, both the antecedent and the consequent are true. . . . A conditional proposition, then, is an assertion of a sequence (and nothing else), and is true if this sequence is valid.[4]

Accordingly, the special rules governing a valid conditional syllogism are: (1) we may posit[5] the antecedent in the minor premise and posit the consequent in the conclusion, (2) or

2 On these rules, *see* Vincent Smith, *The Elements of Logic* (Milwaukee: The Bruce Publishing Company, 1956), pp. 130–136.

3 These laws are: (1) if the antecedent is true and the sequence valid, the consequent is true; (2) if the consequent is false and the sequence valid, the antecedent is false. Complete individual proofs for each law are given by Bachhuber in his *Introduction to Logic* (New York: Appleton-Century-Crofts, Inc., 1957), pp. 138–140.

4 Bachhuber, *op. cit.*, pp. 142–143.

5 To *posit* a member of a hypothetical proposition is to assert it as true (cf. Andrew H. Bachhuber, S.J., *op. cit.*, p. 144).

we may sublate[6] the consequent in the minor premise and sublate the antecedent in the conclusion. Because the major premise of the disjunctive syllogism sets forth alternatives from which the minor premise makes a selection, the special rule governing a valid disjunctive syllogism is the following: the denial of one alternative by the minor premise justifies the affirmation of the other, or of the others; the assertion of one alternative by the minor premise justifies the denial of the other, or of the others. Also, since the major premise of the conjunctive syllogism denies the simultaneous possibility of alternatives, the special rule governing a valid conjunctive syllogism is: if the minor premise asserts one alternative of the major premise, the conclusion must deny the other alternative or alternatives.

VALID FORMS OF THE CATEGORICAL SYLLOGISM

The validity of a categorical syllogism depends upon the clearness and forcefulness with which the decision follows from the premises. This in turn depends upon (1) the position which the middle term holds in the premises, known as the "figure" of the syllogism (because the middle term can assume four different positions in the premises, there are four syllogistic figures); and (2) the disposition of the premises according to quality (the positive or negative character of the copula) and quantity (the distribution of the subject term), called the "mood" of the syllogism. Since this does not appear to be the place to go into all the figures and moods of the syllogism, we shall merely present the valid forms of the categorical syllogism. The reader who wishes further information on this subject may consult any standard reference work in logic.

If all the possible combinations of premises based upon figures and moods are set out, it will be found that the rules given above for the categorical syllogism immediately eliminate as invalid a number of these combinations. These rules

---

6 To *sublate* a member of a hypothetical proposition is to deny it by asserting its contradictory (cf. Andrew H. Bachhuber, S.J., *op. cit.*, p. 144).

are sufficient for ascertaining the validity of any categorical syllogism. If a syllogism violates none of these rules, it is valid. These rules may thus be looked upon as the tests for a good categorical syllogism.

Based upon the figures and moods of the syllogism, there are some 256 combinations of premises. By eliminating those combinations which violate the rules of the syllogism, only 15 combinations or valid forms emerge.[7] These are found in the following chart.

VALID FORMS OF THE CATEGORICAL SYLLOGISM*

	Figure I	Figure II	Figure III	Figure** IV†
Major Premise	A E A E	E A E A	I A O E	A I E††
Minor Premise	A A I I	A E I O	A I A I	E A I
Conclusion	A E I O	E E O O	I I O O	E I O

*Source: A. Ambrose and Morris Lazerowitz, *Fundamentals of Symbolic Logic* (New York: Rinehart and Co., Inc., 1948), p. 265.

**The figure of a syllogism refers to the position which the middle term holds in the premises. In Figure I the middle term is the subject of the major premise and the predicate of the minor premise; in Figure II the middle term is predicate in both premises; in Figure III the middle term is the subject in both premises; in Figure IV the middle term is the predicate of the major premise and the subject of the minor premise.

†The question as to whether the celebrated fourth figure provides a true syllogism has been a matter of some debate among logicians. Because the problem is too complicated to be treated in a discussion of applied logic, the writer refers the interested reader to Jacques Maritain's *Formal Logic* (New York: Sheed and Ward, 1946), pp. 186–192.

††The four traditional types of categorical premises are customarily designated as follows: as follows: *A* stands for the universal affirmative (the subject term of the premise is distributed — it includes *all* members of its class — and the copula — some form of the verb "to be" — is positive); *E* for the universal negative (the subject term is distributed and the copula is negative); *I* for the particular affirmative (the subject term is undistributed — it includes only *some* members of its class — and the copula is positive); and *O* for the particular negative (the subject term is undistributed and the copula is negative).

This chart may now be gainfully used as a basis for demonstrating the 15 valid forms. The following examples, with middle terms set in italics, are verbal illustrations of the four valid forms of Figure I:

A — *Decision-making* causes emotional stimulation.
A — Choosing from among alternatives is *decision-making*.
A — Choosing from among alternatives causes emotional stimulation.

E — *Good executives* are not authoritarians.
A — Human relaters are *good executives*.
E — No human relaters are authoritarians.

⁷ A. Ambrose and Morris Lazerowitz, *Fundamentals of Symbolic Logic* (New York: Rinehart and Co., Inc., 1948), p. 268.

A — *Hoarders of capital* are misers.
I — Some managers are *hoarders of capital*.
I — Some managers are misers.

E — *Dishonest men* will not prosper.
I — Some supervisors are *dishonest men*.
O — Some supervisors will not prosper.

In the foregoing examples and in those that follow it should be recalled what was said earlier in the present chapter about deduction: if the premises are true, then the conclusion is valid and true; if the premises are false, then the conclusion is valid but false. In other words, the decision-maker cannot get more out of his premises than is contained therein.

Now for an example of each of the valid forms of Figure II:

E — Poor people are not *moneylenders*.
A — Bankers are *moneylenders*.
E — Bankers are not poor people.

A — All managers are *rational*.
E — No brutes are *rational*.
E — No brutes are managers.

E — No real decision-makers lack *imagination*.
I — Some executives lack *imagination*.
O — Some executives are not real decision-makers.

A — All fine art is *beautiful*.
O — Some music is not *beautiful*.
O — Some music is not fine art.

The next four examples illustrate how syllogisms can be validly constructed according to Figure III:

I — Some *brokers* are intellectuals.
A — All *brokers* are wealthy.
I — Some wealthy are intellectual.

A — All *brokers* are wealthy.
I — Some *brokers* are intellectuals.
I — Some intellectuals are wealthy.

O — Some *executives* are not trustworthy.
A — All *executives* are decision-makers.
O — Some decision-makers are not trustworthy.

E — No *administrators* are spendthrifts.
I — Some *administrators* are intellectuals.
O — Some intellectuals are not spendthrifts.

Finally, for examples of the valid forms of Figure IV, the following are submitted:

A — All facts are *universals*.
E — No *universals* are opinions.
E — No opinions are facts.

I — Some decision-makers are *spirited creatures*.
A — All *spirited creatures* are difficult to manage.
I — Some creatures difficult to manage are decision-makers.

E — No dishonest men are *prosperous men*.
I — Some *prosperous men* are supervisors.
O — Some supervisors are not dishonest men.

Thus, upon examination of the foregoing examples in each of the above four figures it is clearly seen that in the categorical syllogism the middle term is the *cause* of valid reasoning and it is the key to the categorical syllogism. In this case, good reasoning is actually the search for good middle terms. So much then for the valid forms of the categorical syllogism. Let us now turn to the valid forms of the other major form of deduction — the hypothetical syllogism.

VALID FORMS OF THE HYPOTHETICAL SYLLOGISM

Like the valid forms of the categorical syllogism, those of the hypothetical syllogism are based upon the rules cited above for the three forms of hypothetical syllogisms: the conditional, the disjunctive, and the conjunctive syllogisms. Both the valid and invalid forms of the hypothetical syllogism are presented in the chart on p. 69. The following examples are submitted as illustrative of the valid and invalid forms of the conditional syllogism.

	If you are a good decision-maker, then you are a good manager.
(1) Valid:	But you are a good decision-maker.
	Therefore, you are a good manager.

If you are a good decision-maker, then you are a good manager.

(2) Valid: But you are not a good manager.

Therefore, you are not a good decision-maker.

If you are a good decision-maker, then you are a good manager.

3 — Invalid: But you are a good manager.

Therefore, you are a good decision-maker.

If you are a good decision-maker, then you are a good manager.

4 — Invalid: But you are not a good decision-maker.

Therefore, you are not a good manager.

The next four examples illustrate the valid and invalid forms of the disjunctive syllogism in the strict sense:

Either you are a good decision-maker, or you are a poor decision-maker.

(1) Valid: But you are a good decision-maker.

Therefore, you are not a poor decision-maker.

Either you are a good decision-maker, or you are a poor decision-maker.

(2) Valid: But you are not a good decision-maker.

Therefore, you are a poor decision-maker.

Either you are a good decision-maker, or you are a poor decision-maker.

3 — Invalid: But you are a good decision-maker.

Therefore, you are a poor decision-maker.

Either you are a good decision-maker, or you are a poor decision-maker.

4 — Invalid: But you are not a good decision-maker.

Therefore, you are not a poor decision-maker.

Now, for an example of each of the valid and invalid forms of the disjunctive syllogism in the broad sense:

Either you are a good decision-maker, or you are a poor manager.

(1) Valid: But you are not a good decision-maker.

Therefore, you are a poor manager.

Either you are a good decision-maker, or you are a poor manager.

2 — Invalid: But you are a good decision-maker.

Therefore, you are not a poor manager.

VALID AND INVALID FORMS OF THE
HYPOTHETICAL SYLLOGISM*

Major Premise	Minor Premise (Categorical)		Conclusion
Conditional proposition	VALID	(1) POSIT ANTECEDENT (2) SUBLATE CONSEQUENT	POSIT CONSE- QUENT SUBLATE ANTECEDENT
("If A, then B")	invalid	3 — posit consequent 4 — sublate antecedent	posit antecedent sublate consequent
Disjunctive proposition in strict sense ("Either A, or B, but not both")	VALID	(1) POSIT ONE MEMBER (2) SUBLATE ONE (OR MORE) OF MEMBERS	SUBLATE EACH OF THE OTHERS POSIT OTHER(S WITH STRICT DISJUNCTIVE)
	invalid	3 — posit one member 4 — sublate one member	posit another sublate all the others
Disjunctive proposition in broad sense ("Either A, or B, maybe both.")	VALID	(1) SUBLATE ONE (OR MORE BUT NOT ALL) OF THE MEMBERS	POSIT OTHER(S WITH BROAD DISJUNCTIVE)
	invalid	2 — posit one member	sublate another
Conjunctive proposition ("Not both A and B, maybe neither.")	VALID	(1) POSIT ONE MEMBER	SUBLATE THE OTHER
	invalid	2 — sublate one member	posit the other

*Source: Andrew H. Bachhuber, S.J., *Introduction to Logic* (New York: Appleton-Century-Crofts, Inc., 1957), p. 159.
Note: To posit a member of a hypothetical proposition is to assert it as true; to sublate a member of a hypothetical proposition is to deny it by asserting its contradictory. In the rules for the conclusion, the part enclosed in parentheses states what is to be done if the major premise is a disjunctive proposition of more than two members.

Finally, for examples of the valid and invalid forms of the conjunctive syllogism:

(1) Valid:
> The general manager cannot be in Chicago and Detroit at the same time.
> But the general manager is now in Chicago.
> Therefore, the general manager cannot now be in Detroit.

2 — Invalid:
> The general manager cannot be in Chicago and Detroit at the same time.
> But the general manager is not now in Chicago.
> Therefore, the general manager is now in Detroit.

Accordingly, it is seen from an investigation of the foregoing examples of the hypothetical syllogism that valid reasoning with respect to the conditional syllogism depends very much upon the relationship of the antecedent to its consequent. In the disjunctive and conjunctive syllogisms, good reasoning depends greatly upon the assertion made in the minor premise with respect to the alternatives presented in the major premise.

The valid forms of the hypothetical syllogism plus the valid forms of the categorical syllogism together comprise the valid forms of deduction. The value and use of the categorical and the hypothetical syllogisms to the decision-maker will be demonstrated in the next chapter — Chapter 9.

9 LOGICAL ANALYSIS IN DECISION-MAKING — A DEMONSTRATION

WE HAVE now finished our study of the theory of logic; but by far the most important and most neglected part still remains to be treated. It seems utterly vain and useless to know the principles of logic if we do not employ them for the end for which they were intended. Especially in this does the present treatise differ from others. This is, in truth, the all-important point in studying and learning the laws of logic. It is of little value to know the rules of any science or art, unless we reduce them to practice.

Up to the present, we have attempted to learn something about the logical stages of decision-making, premises as antecedents of decision, decision and implication, the logical properties of premises, induction and deduction. Our demonstration, then, will take place within the framework of the four logical stages of decision-making. We have learned that stage 1 — a feeling of uncertainty or doubt — depends upon the state of development of a manager's conceptual structure. A well-developed conceptual framework is sensitive to challenging problems. On the other hand, a less well-constructed system of ideas may fail to provide the necessary awareness of a problem and the accompanying uncertainty as to what to do about it. In the case of The Chicago Metal Company,[1] Mr. Willis

---

[1] The Chicago Metal Company, a case problem which appears in the appendix to this chapter on pp. 78–82, should now be carefully studied and analyzed. The Chicago Metal Company is an actual business case with the name of the company and the names of all the individuals concerned disguised, and will be used to demonstrate the relevance of the contributions of logical method to managerial decision-making. Although The Chicago Metal Company is an industrial case, any kind of case could have been used, be it in public administration, nonprofit organizations, hospitals, the military, etc. This is so

possesses such a sufficiently sensitive conceptual structure because, prior to undertaking his new assignment, he anticipates a future situation that is characterized by changes and problems. His reflections regarding these changes and problems indicate that he is experiencing a feeling of uncertainty or doubt. It is precisely because Mr. Willis is aware of a problem that he feels uncertain. Now it is in this stage 1 — the stage of uncertainty — that background in the science of logic is indispensable. Each decision-maker possesses a body of ideas, concepts, or principles which he has developed through experience and study. These principles are premises upon which the decision-maker rests his present deliberation; that is, it is against these premises that he continually compares what he finds in a business situation, and it is upon these premises that the decision-maker bases his judgment that a particular business situation is "problematic." Since this process of reasoning begins with principles as premises and proceeds to a judgment, it must be called deduction, even though it is, perhaps, almost always done informally.

Stimulated by a feeling of uncertainty or doubt, Mr. Willis investigates the problematic situation to reach a clear understanding of the problem. In stage 2 — the stage of analysis and definition — Mr. Willis seeks to discover the relevant facts in order that the problem may be defined. Many judgments will be required in evaluating the numerous facts which demand interpretation in the second stage of decision-making. The decision-maker is searching for relevancy in regard to each fact studied, and this involves his judgment that a certain fact bears on his original feeling of uncertainty. Poor judgment will lead to the inclusion of many facts that have no bearing on the case and will thus tend to obscure the issues at stake. Here again logic will contribute in the same way as it does in the first stage. Thus, each decision

---

because decision-making is essentially the same process anywhere. The only thing that changes is the subject matter to which the process is applied, not the process itself.

to include or exclude a certain fact will be the result of at least informal syllogistic reasoning; that is, the fact at hand will be joined to a proposition that expresses the manager's concept of the origin of his doubt and the conclusion will reject or accept the fact as relevant. Upon careful analysis, Mr. Willis discloses the following relevant facts:

1. Decision-making power has historically been centralized in the home office. The plant manager now possesses many times more discretionary power than in the past.
2. The organization has had a strong informal system of relationships in the past.
3. Profits are declining; competition is increasing.
4. Lower costs, reduced labor requirements, and improved uniformity of product quality are some of the goals top management is looking for from the experiment.
5. Management has taken the view that some form of relationship between the home office production staff and the plant manager be retained, but only after a previous split on the issue, and finally with the qualification that the final decision be made by Mr. Willis.
6. Mr. Willis is charged with full responsibility for the success of the decentralized operation.
7. Top management has substantial confidence in the ability of Mr. Willis.[2]

Based upon the foregoing relevant facts, the following is submitted as a statement of the specific problem facing Mr. Willis: By means of what organizational plan can Mr. Willis achieve effective control in the new operation so that the top management goals of reduced labor and other costs, and improved uniformity of product quality may be realized? Here is a clear example of induction — of making the "induc-

---

[2] As indicated in Chapter 3, the disclosure of relevant facts is dominated to a great extent by the conceptual structure that the decision-maker brings to the facts. Since the statement of the problem significantly depends upon the factual analysis, it is in turn affected by one's system of ideas. Moreover, emotional bias, habit or traditional behavior, and seeking the road of least resistance affect the statement of the problem. Consequently, the reader should not be disturbed if he does not agree with the writer's statement of the problem or the relevant facts. Whatever the relevant facts or the problem, the method is unchanged and still applies.

tive assent" from a number of instances or particulars (the relevant facts cited above) to a more general statement (the definition of the problem).

Having investigated the facts and clearly stated the problem with reference to the desired goals, the decision-maker begins to develop possible alternatives. These alternatives are tentative solutions to the problem and are preliminary judgments that certain actions will achieve certain results. In the very act of suggesting a solution the manager must have reasoned, at least informally, that on the assumption of this or that premise together with this or that fact or facts, such a conclusion is valid. If he doesn't proceed in this manner, his alternatives will neither be reasonable nor pertinent. Again, the possession of such premises from which conclusions can be inferred is directly related to the conceptual framework of the manager which, as has been said, is a product of experience and study. Wherever judgment and reasoning are needed, it is also necessary to know the rules governing them, and these are the contribution of logic.

The problem statement of stage 2 plus the relevant facts plus our previous knowledge may now be used to suggest relevant alternatives — stage 3. After considerable mental activity, directed by the objective set up in the problem statement, Mr. Willis may offer the following alternatives, hypotheses, or tentative solutions:

(1) Use the proposed organizational structure (Exhibit II).
(2) Use a plan of organizational structure with no divided authority (Exhibit II without the broken lines).
(3) Use any other plan of organizational structure.[3]

In the final stage of the process a choice must be made among the possible alternatives proposed in the third stage. To do this each will have to be examined carefully and all

---

[3] This alternative is a universal one to stand for any or all possible alternatives the reader may think of. Since the writer would achieve nothing except complexity by listing say twelve alternatives instead of three, it was thought best to keep the demonstration as simple as possible but yet adequate to illustrate the method.

but one rejected as not being the best solution to the problem. In this area it is especially easy to jump to unwarranted conclusions. To avoid this pitfall each alternative must be treated deductively; that is, the assumption involved in the alternatives must be stated and the reasoning analyzed, first, for its ⟨validity⟩ and, second, for its ⟨truth.⟩ In the area of validity, logic will point the way but in the area of truth other fields of knowledge must join hands with logic to supply the answer.

With the alternatives proposed, Mr. Willis must now treat them deductively — stage 4. It is in this stage — the stage of verification — that the logician makes his cardinal contribution to decision-making. To treat an alternative deductively involves syllogistic reasoning. Accordingly, Mr. Willis may formally commence his logical reasoning process by setting up the following hypothetical syllogism:

> Either the proposed organizational structure will yield control, or a plan of organizational structure with no divided authority will yield control.
> But the proposed organizational structure will yield control (because it has the support of top management).
> Therefore, a plan of organizational structure with no divided authority will not yield control.

This argument is a valid hypothetical syllogism of the disjunctive type. It may be employed, as here, to eliminate suggested solutions of problems.[4] In this case, Mr. Willis has used it to negate his suggested alternative 2. The disjunctive syllogism may similarly be used to eliminate alternative 3 as follows:

Either the proposed organizational structure will yield control

---

4 A more informal approach to the elimination of certain alternatives is the simple listing of the advantages or disadvantages, that is, the desirable and undesirable consequences of each alternative in an attempt to discover the alternative with the largest aggregate of desirable consequences. If the decision-maker wishes to retain this approach within the framework of the four stages of decision-making, then the advantages and disadvantages should preferably be listed with the related alternatives as a part of stage 3.

or any other plan of organizational structure will yield
control.
But the proposed organizational structure will yield control
(because it has the support of top management).
Therefore, any other plan of organizational structure will not
yield control.

The elimination of alternatives 2 and 3 does not, however,
establish the truth of alternative 1. Alternative 1 must be
formally established. Therefore, Mr. Willis must reason further. He may then develop the following hypothetical syllogism with respect to his alternative 1:

If the proposed organizational structure has the support of
top management, then it will yield control.
But the proposed organizational structure has the support of
top management.
Therefore, the proposed organizational structure will yield
control.

This is a valid hypothetical syllogism of the conditional type.
It formally establishes the validity of alternative 1.

From the foregoing analysis, Mr. Willis may decide that
he should adopt alternative 1. He should realize, however,
that although his process of logical reasoning has established
the validity of alternative 1, the truth of his conclusions
depends upon the truth of his premises. Unfortunately, logic
is no protection against error in the formulation of the
premises. Yet, Mr. Willis is much better off at this stage
than he would be if he used no logic. If he used no logic,
he could not even be sure of a valid reasoning process, and
consequently his decisions could be both untrue and invalid.
Indeed, invalid decisions possess a quality not possessed by
valid decisions — there is no possibility that invalid decisions
are true, unless they are true independently of the premises.
This means that the apparent premises and decisions are not
related to one another at all. On the other hand, a valid
decision resulting from a valid reasoning process has, at least,
a possibility of being true. It follows, consequently, that very

careful attention must be directed to the formation of the premises, if decisions are to be true as well as logically valid. But the administrator is primarily interested not in the validity of his decision but rather in its truth. To establish the truth of the above decision that Mr. Willis should adopt alternative 1, further analysis is necessary. The second premise (minor) of the above conditional syllogism can be established by observation (of the relevant facts of the situation) and induction. The first premise (major), however, is not so easily verified. Here the categorical syllogism can play a vital role. For example, Mr. Willis could set up the following categorical syllogisms:

> Final authority rests with top management.
> Efficient organizational structures are based upon final authority.
> Therefore, efficient organizational structures rest with top management.

then,

> The support of top management will yield control.
> The proposed organizational structure has the support of top management.
> Therefore, the proposed organizational structure will yield control.

These categorical syllogisms are valid forms from Figure I. They are of the AAA and AII variety respectively. The major premises in the above categorical syllogisms are in the nature of principles of management or administration. Mr. Willis, being a prudent man, will avail himself of all the principles of administration, economics, and other relevant sciences which he has at his command before coming to his final decision. Accordingly, the first and fourth premises in the above categorical syllogisms will be statements of what Mr. Willis believes to be sound and true principles. If they are not, then his search for truth will reap no harvest this time (we hope he will adjust his principles for the future as he discovers that they are not true). On the other hand, if the first and fourth propositions are true (and Mr. Willis has to go on the assumption that they are), then the conclusion of the conditional syllogism is not only valid but also true. Consequently, Mr. Willis should adopt alternative 1.

APPENDIX TO CHAPTER 9

The Chicago Metal Company

A CASE STUDY

The Chicago Metal Company is a large metal manufacturing company with twelve plants scattered throughout various parts of the United States. Each plant employs from 500 to 1000 persons.

The home office of the company is in downtown Chicago, commonly called the Loop. The chief executive officers of the company are located in the home office on State Street. These include the president, the executive vice-president, and the vice-presidents in charge of sales, production, procurement, finance, and control (accounting). Moreover, the vice-president in charge of production has a manufacturing staff reporting to him, composed of the assistant vice-presidents of engineering, production control, quality control, and methods. Representatives of each of the home-office staff are located in each plant, and they are directly responsible to the plant manager as well as to their respective staff superiors in the home office (Exhibit I). Formally, this amounted to divided authority; but, in practice, the plant manager had little authority on an operating basis.

Since the company's founding in 1935 in a small shop on the far south side of Chicago, decision-making power has been highly centralized in the home office. As a matter of fact, in the past, plant managers had no knowledge and received no notification of company plans until the production orders were already on their desk. The personnel of the plant feel that the best place to make operating decisions is as close to the operating activities as possible. Consequently,

Exhibit I

THE CHICAGO METAL COMPANY
PARTIAL PRESENT ORGANIZATION

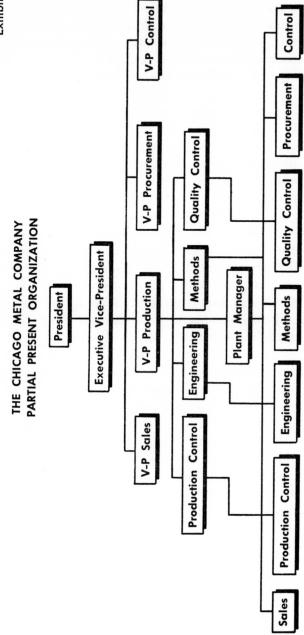

there was frequently friction between the home-office representatives and the plant personnel.

For several years now the company has not been satisfied with profits, as competition seems to be getting keener. As an experiment, the home-office executive committee, which consists of all the executives in the Chicago office (Exhibit I), recently approved the use of one of the company's modern plants to be operated on a somewhat decentralized basis. Top management has decided to put the claims of the plant people to the test. Because new production methods would be employed, lower fabricating costs, reduced labor requirements, and improved uniformity of product quality are some of the goals top management anticipates from the new operation.

The man appointed to be manager of the new operation is Mr. George Willis. Mr. Willis has been with the company for six years in various capacities in engineering, production and quality control, and methods. Before joining The Chicago Metal Company, Mr. Willis spent ten years as an accountant with a number of firms, ultimately holding the position of controller before coming to The Chicago Metal Company. While practicing accounting, Mr. Willis matriculated at the University of Chicago and received his Master of Business Administration degree in production management just before joining the The Chicago Metal Company. Anxious to get into production management, Mr. Willis has literally been a bundle of energy giving everything he has while at The Chicago Metal Company. His demonstrated managerial ability plus his reputation as a cost finder and a cost reducer, plus the fact that he is also a good man in human relations, seemed to get him the support necessary to be appointed manager of the pilot operation.

Although delighted with his new and challenging assignment, Mr. Willis is not unaware of the problems facing him. He realizes that a new experiment such as The Chicago Metal Company is undertaking after so many years under the former central control of manufacturing operations is going to create

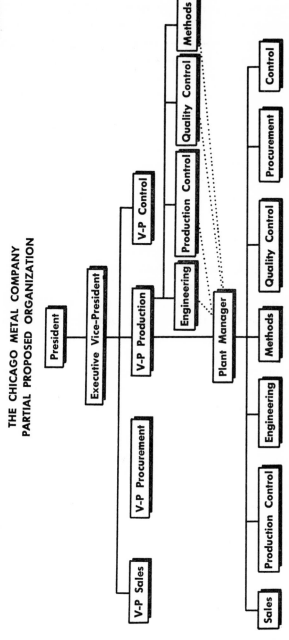

Exhibit II

THE CHICAGO METAL COMPANY
PARTIAL PROPOSED ORGANIZATION

major changes and problems. He will have a modern plant, new processes, new methods, new people, and new organizational relationships. Previously, the plant manager dealt with the appropriate staff representation; if no satisfactory agreement was reached, he went upstairs to the vice-president of production. Now, the plant manager is vested with many times more discretionary power than before, and he may deal directly with the vice-president of production.

At the final meeting of the home-office executive committee concerning organization, a difference of opinion developed. The vice-presidents of sales, procurement, production, and control wished to have all relationships between the home office and the plant manager cut off except for the pure line relationship of the plant manager to the vice-president of production. The assistant staff of the vice-president of production at the home office (engineering, production control, quality control, methods) felt, however, that some sort of staff or functional (line) relationship between them and the plant manager should be retained (Exhibit II). Because the home-office staff of the vice-president of production felt so strongly about retaining some form of direct hierarchical relationship with the new plant manager, and since they were all production people, the remaining members of the executive committee decided, after considerable discussion, to go along with them. However, they did so only on condition that Mr. Willis be given final authority to decide upon the organizational relationships, since he is the one responsible for the success of the decentralization experiment. This was agreed to and the meeting terminated.

10 CONCLUSIONS

CHAPTERS 3 through 9 have been concerned with an investigation into the relevant contributions of logical method to the intellectual activity of decision-making. This inquiry was launched on the premise that, in spite of the extraordinary significance of decision-making to managers, the subject has, until recently, received relatively little attention, and is a management activity that remains largely *terra incognita*, especially in the field of top management. With the business scene becoming more and more complex in the era of automation, the time is now ripe for top management to put its decision-making on a more intellectually rational basis. As a matter of fact, in spite of the determined opposition of its adherents, the "rule-of-thumb" approach is already obsolete in some segments of United States industry.

Phenomenologically speaking, many business managers generally are more interested in results than in the methods whereby the results are obtained. Their first impulse is to accept the plausible as true and to reject the uncongenial as false. They have neither the time nor the inclination to investigate. Indeed, the call to do so is often felt as irksome. Furthermore, when they are asked to treat their "cherished beliefs" as mere hypotheses, they rebel violently.

Moreover, intuitionists are ceaselessly at work trying to undermine respect for more rational processes of decision-making. These attacks have always met with wide acclaim and are bound to continue to be met in this way, for they strike a responsive note in human nature. Unfortunately, they do not offer any reliable alternative method for obtaining sound decisions. Intuition may appear to give managers subjective certainty, but can give no proof that contrary intuitions are erroneous.

Making use of the relevant contributions of logical method, on the other hand, is a way of minimizing arbitrary opinion. It is well to clarify our ideas by asking for the precise meaning of our words, and to try to check our "favorite ideas" by applying them to accurately formulated propositions. To a really good manager, whose I.Q. is far above the average, syllogistic deductions may be so obvious and take place so quickly that he may scarcely be aware of their existence. But not everybody can have an I.Q. so far above the mean. Hence for most administrators there is a psychological problem of making correct deductions.

No sensible person who has at his command the techniques of logical manipulation would knowingly tackle a difficult problem without using them. Logic's test of internal consistency and the convenience of logic for handling deductive inferences are indisputable. Of course, to say that managers trained in logic will not make mistakes is going too far. But it is encouraging to note that sound logic will help insure valid steps in carrying out the deductive process. Where the really big mistakes are made is in the formulation of premises. Logic, unfortunately, is no protection against the misinterpretation of empirical reality. One of the advantages of the logical medium is, however, that we are forced to lay our cards on the table so that we can see our premises.

Yet the "suspension of judgment" which is essential to decision-making is difficult or impossible when we are pressed by the demands of "immediate action." When my house is on fire, I must act quickly and promptly — I cannot stop to consider the possible causes, nor even to estimate the consequences involved in the various alternative ways of reacting. Similarly, when the business situation calls for an immediate decision, it is frequently better for the executive to risk being wrong than to risk a delay. For this reason, those who are bent upon some specific course of action often despise those devoted to reflection; and some even seem to argue as though the need for action guaranteed the truth of their decision. Furthermore, none of the precautions of the logical method can prevent business life or personal life from being an adventure. But the logical method does enable large numbers to walk with surer steps. By analyzing the possibilities of alternative hypotheses, it becomes possible to anticipate outcomes and adjust ourselves in advance. Logical method, while no panacea, thus minimizes the shock of novelty and the uncertainty of decision-making. It enables us to frame policies of action fit for a wider outlook than those of immediate physical stimulus or organic response.

Specifically, then, the syllogism, which is the chief contribution of the logical method, serves the decision-maker in two very important capacities. It performs the indispensable function of serving as a means of testing an alternative. As such, the syllogism may be considered a generalized formula for logical conditions that must be satisfied if an alternative is to be accepted as valid. In other words, the utility of the syllogistic form resides in the fact that it serves as a check in the case of decisions, holding up the logical conditions to be satisfied. Second, it may be used to suggest experimental combinations of premises. That is, the decision-maker may take a premise and combine it with others to see where the reasoning will lead him (the conclusion in one syllogism may become a premise in another syllogism and so on). The process need not necessarily be strictly valid (as when a categorical syllogism has an undistributed middle term) because the decision is usually only probable anyway. It is a serious misunderstanding of the syllogism to make a dictator of it in decision-making, where probable decisions have great practical significance. This points up the importance of having some awareness of the theory of the syllogism; if the decision-maker understands the syllogism he will know when he deviates from the theory as well as when he does not, and consequently he will not expect his decisions to be any better than the process he used to arrive at them. Accordingly, in the light of the foregoing, it appears that the logician's effective use of the syllogism has its counterpart in the decision-maker's demonstrated functional use of the same abbreviated mode of deduction. Actually, whether it be the logician or the decision-maker who is using the syllogistic form, the veracity of the process is the same, for a syllogism is like a spotlight probing the insecure fastenings of every administrative or personal decision.

CASES FOR ANALYSIS AND DECISION

INTRODUCTION TO THE CASES

THE objective of this section is to provide the reader with ample opportunity to develop a logical method of thinking in real-life situations. The "case method" has proven invaluable by adding realism, practicality, and participation to the learning process. Through his own analysis of the problematic situation and the evidence, the decision-maker reaches his own decisions. By repetition in solving a number of cases, the reader learns to look at singular situations objectively and to develop logically sound decisions. Moreover, if the reader believes that the method propounded in the first part of this book has any value, then by diligently attempting to solve these cases within the framework of the four stages of decision-making, the method will soon become a part of his personal equipment. As such, this sharpened tool will be ready for immediate use when required for making decisions.

No questions are presented at the end of each case. The writer feels that the greatest value can be achieved if the reader will undertake his own analysis of each case and its facts, define the problem, formulate several alternatives, test and verify the alternatives, and then make his final decision. If the reader wishes a model, he may follow the detailed demonstration in Chapter 9.

The author recognizes that people work in all sorts of organizations, not only in business organizations. Accordingly, although the majority of the cases are business cases, there is also included one case in public administration (The City of Industry), one in hospital administration (The South Shore Hospital), one in social service administration (Social Services, Inc.), and one in business association management (Automobile Manufacturers Association). Except for the Ford Motor Company, Ex-Cell-O Corporation, McLouth Steel Corporation, and the Automobile Manufacturers Association, the names of the cases and the names of all individuals are fictitious; however, all the situations are real and represent actual situations. The factual information has been compiled from sources of repute, although not infallible. The accuracy and completeness of the information are not, therefore, guaranteed and it is not intended that the information be used as the basis for investment decisions or any other decisions outside of demonstrations in decision-making.

Finally, no one would deny that the decisions of major companies are of vital concern to the economy of a country; yet, it is important to remember that the majority of decisions are not made by top executives of the large companies. They are made by the owners and managers of small businesses. There are in any community a great variety and number of small businesses. The men who have the responsibility for the successful operation of these businesses are faced with the task of making decisions, each of which may not be so important, taking the national economy as a whole, but which is quite significant for the individual small business and for the families that depend upon the successful management of that business. The decisions that these businessmen make are, therefore, of singular importance for their firms, for their dependents, and ultimately for society as a whole. This is the justification for the inclusion of several "small business" cases among the group of cases that follows.

I. FORD MOTOR COMPANY

On May 18, 1953, the Product Planning Committee of the Ford Motor Company convened to review proposals for Ford's entry into the sports-car market. The Product Planning Committee established by the Board of Directors had authority to take the following action:

1. Approve new vehicle programs subject to the concurrence of the Administration Committee and the Board of Directors.
2. Give final approval to styling details of new model programs.

As constituted in 1953, the Product Planning Committee was essentially coincident with the Administration Committee and with the Board of Directors (except for the public members of the Board who were a minority). Consequently, the limitations imposed upon the authority of the Product Planning Committee were commonly considered to be organizational formalities only.

A sports car may be variously defined, but the following characteristics were generally accepted at the time of the May, 1953, meeting:

1. High performance in both acceleration and top speed.
2. Restricted seating capacity — generally limited to provision for only two persons with comfort.
3. Excellent handling and roadability.
4. Light weight.
5. "Racy," low-slung styling with minimum ornamentation.
6. Compromised passenger comfort and convenience to meet the other objectives. Commonly sports cars as imported from European manufacturers lacked such common American car features as side glass and provision for high-volume options such as an automatic transmission, power steering, and power brakes.

Engineering, Styling, and Product Planning activities at Ford had been studying a possible Ford sports car since 1950. Early studies were quite general and informal and were based largely upon the belief of Ford management that the expanding American income, the rising standard of living, the move to suburban areas, and the increase in two-car families would lead to increasing demand for "specialty" vehicles such as the station wagon, the convertible, and, perhaps, a sports car.

By early 1952 previous opinions regarding the growth of a sports-car market were confirmed by the steadily increasing sales of imported sports cars in America. Unit sales of foreign sports cars had doubled each year since 1949 with sales for 1952 projected at around 12,000 units (see Exhibit I). In addition, domestic manufacturers were introducing dream cars and special sports models at automobile shows and in limited production to judge public reaction to advanced engineering and styling features. One other factor contributed to the Ford Motor Company's increasing interest in the sports-car market in 1952. The associa-

Exhibit I

SPORTS CAR REGISTRATIONS*
1952

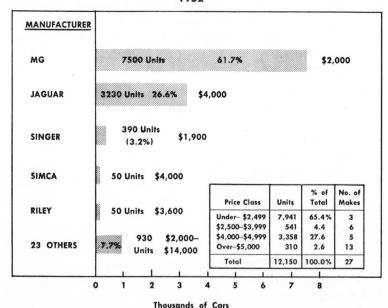

Price Class	Units	% of Total	No. of Makes
Under– $2,499	7,941	65.4%	3
$2,500–$3,999	541	4.4	6
$4,000–$4,999	3,358	27.6	5
Over–$5,000	310	2.6	13
Total	12,150	100.0%	27

Thousands of Cars

*Based on 11 months' data.

tion of the Ford car with the model "T" remained a strong one in the minds of many of the buying public. Consumer research studies showed that this association implied economy, trustworthiness, reliability, and simplicity to many car buyers. Also implied, however, were unfavorable images such as commonness, discomfort, unprogressiveness, and lack of beauty. An advanced Ford sports car was considered to have the potential of remaking the public image of the Ford car by destroying those unfavorable lingering impressions which remained with the car-buying public from the still well-remembered earlier Ford successes.

In October, 1952, the Ford Motor Company recognized that the above factors indicated the possibility of a successful Ford-produced sports car and launched expanded studies of the problem. The Engineering Staff reviewed the characteristics of all existing sports cars to arrive at package, performance, and other specifications which would permit a Ford-produced sports car to equal or better the performance of expensive imported foreign models. As an initial objective, performance at least equal to the popular and highly regarded English-made Jaguar XK-120 was established as a goal. Package dimensions similar to the Jaguar were also selected and transmitted to Styling where ⅜ scale clay models were begun. The Merchandising and Product Planning Office of the Ford Division initiated market research studies and began preliminary cost-price-profit analyses at various possible sales volumes.

On February 9, 1953, the Ford Division presented its preliminary plans for a sports car to the Product Planning Committee and requested the concurrence of the Committee in the following program:

1. Development of a full-sized clay model.
2. Determination of firm estimates for design, tooling, and manufacturing cost and final sourcing plans.
3. Presentation to the Product Planning Committee of the clay model and firm estimates of the cost factors involved prior to a final decision committing the Company to enter the sports-car field.

The Committee approved the proposed Ford Division program, which was based on the information presented and on estimated expenditures, to complete the study by approximately May 1,

1953. Pertinent excerpts from the February presentation are as follows:

Introduction

Cars referred to as sports-car types may be generally grouped in two categories:

1. THE TRUE SPORTS CAR — typified by the MG and the Jaguar — generally a two-passenger roadster or convertible with long, low proportions and little exterior ornamentation.
2. THE "SPORTS LIKE" CAR — is unlike the true sports car in that it may be closely identified with standard passenger cars. It possesses a few of the unique sports-car characteristics, but relies on rework, trim, and ornamentation to achieve a sports-car effect. In the main, however, standard production components are utilized. Examples of this type vehicle include the Buick Skylark and Packard Caribbean.

The importance of "sports-like" cars has been discussed in connection with the development of the 1955 Fairlane (this has reference to plans to introduce special 1955 models which eventually evolved into the Crown Victorias). The purpose of this review is to outline the possibilities for Ford in the true sports-car field.

Sales and Market Considerations

In order to obtain information on the nature of the sports-car market, a survey was conducted by the Ford Division Consumer Research Department. This survey indicated that people who purchase sports cars are:

1. Automobile-conscious individuals who enjoy driving a "different," highly efficient, sensitive car.
2. Almost unanimous in their intention to repurchase a sports car in the future.
3. Associated with sports-car clubs, although very few actively participate in road racing or other types of road competition.
4. Also owners of conventional cars for general purpose use.
5. In addition, the survey showed the following characteristics of MG and Jaguar owners:

	MG	*Jaguar*
Age	Around 30	Over 35
Marital Status	Single	Married
Annual Income	Under $10,000	Over $10,000
Owner Loyalty	Desire to Upgrade	High level

In summary, our preliminary sales and market analysis indicate that:

1. The market is currently dominated by two cars, the MG and the Jaguar. However, the entry of American manufacturers can be expected to alter this sales distribution substantially.
2. Registration data show that, although the sales volume has doubled each year since 1949, the total volume for 1952 amounted to only 12,000 units. While any sales projection is at best a rough estimate, an industry volume of 25,000 to 50,000 units might be realized with entry of Ford and/or Chevrolet in the field.
3. Buyers desire more of a package than is offered by the small, low-powered MG which sells for approximately $2,000. This is evidenced by their expressed desire to upgrade themselves to the Jaguar, selling for approximately $4,000.
4. A larger more powerful car than the MG, selling in the $3,000–$3,500 range, would enter a segment of the market where little competition exists and would attract buyers in both the low-priced and high-priced class.

Product Requirements

The basic requirements which appear desirable to achieve a sports-car representative of the Ford line may be summarized as follows:

1. A Ford sports car should retain Ford product characteristics and identification to the extent necessary for ready association with the standard production Ford car.
2. It should have as many standard chassis and engine production components as possible in order to minimize costs and to facilitate servicing by Ford dealers.
3. It should be a lightweight vehicle with the performance and roadability characteristics required of a true sports car.

In line with these requirements, Engineering has developed a package size and specifications for a Ford sports car.

Design Objectives

Package Size
1. A two-passenger open model (including canvas top and side curtains).
2. Provide reasonable driver and passenger comfort.

Weight
1. Package designed for minimum weight to obtain high performance.
2. Weight distribution balanced for good roadability.

Performance
1. Acceleration superior to competition.
2. Good high-speed handling characteristics and roadability.

Interchangeability
1. Maximum use of standard production components.

Summary

In summary, Engineering and the Ford Division have conducted a preliminary survey of the possibilities for Ford in the sports-car field from a marketing, product, and cost standpoint. The results of this study indicate that:

1. There is a fast-growing but still small market for this type of vehicle.
2. A Ford-designed vehicle could compete successfully in this field from both a styling and performance standpoint.
3. The chief advantage of entry into the field would be one of prestige.
4. With respect to cost, the proposed design should be one which would:
   a) Enable the car to be built on a self-supporting basis at low volume.
   b) Permit it to be priced in a favorable position.

The financial data included in the presentation indicated a break-even point of 9600 units based upon a tentative $3,500 retail list price (not including excise taxes or delivery charges). This estimate of break-even point was based upon tentative projections of incremental fixed and variable cost which were, of course, extremely preliminary since the vehicle at this time existed only in concept form on paper.[1] In addition to the presentation itself, the minutes of the February 9, 1953, meeting record a discussion in which it was pointed out by the Engineering Staff that consideration should not be given to options such as the automatic transmission, power steering, and power brakes since such equipment was not in accord with the characteristics of a "true sports car."

Subsequent to the February Product Planning Committee meeting, efforts were intensified to resolve final styling, engineering, and merchandising details of the car before the tentative May 1 final review and approval or disapproval of the program. Particular attention was given to the concept of a "true" sports car and its advantages and limitations. A true sports car in the European tradition certainly would have advantages — mainly associated with the hard core of loyal sports-car followers who had already demonstrated their enthusiasm for the unique sports-car appeal. The appeal of the sports car to its fans was at least partly caused by the thrill of manually shifting gears in a high-performance automobile, by the feel of road shock and vibration through a solidly sprung suspension which provided unmatched handling ability, and by the boldness associated with braving the elements in a vehicle which offered only limited protection and always subjected its occupants to the risk of abuse from sudden changes in the weather.

On the other hand, a true sports car styled with traditional sports-car functionalism would be somewhat difficult to identify with the larger Ford products with contemporary American styling. Also a true sports car, because of the same unique features which appeared to be so appealing to sports-car enthusiasts, might have little appeal to the average American car buyer who was showing increasing interest in such features as automatic transmissions, power steering, power brakes, and even power windows and power seats. One of the original major objectives in the sports-car program had been the development of a vehicle which would have wide appeal among car buyers and therefore would permit the remolding of the public image of Ford products along

[1] Volume requirement for break-even on this vehicle is unusually low. It is based on analysis of incremental cost only and does not assume allocation to the new vehicle of a share of the major fixed expenditures on components interchangeable with the high-volume Ford car.

more favored lines. The inherent compromises of a true sports car would be sure to limit its appeal and make the attainment of this objective difficult. It appeared, therefore, that a vehicle in between the true sports car and the American passenger car might have certain advantages, but only at added risk in increased investment and at least a partial abandonment of the ready-made market of "true" sports-car enthusiasts.

Nevertheless, the Ford Division studied this as yet unnamed alternative and first discussed it with the Product Planning Committee at an April 27, 1953, meeting in which a review of progress on sports-car clay models had been scheduled. The Product Planning Committee at that time requested that detailed plans and financial data on this alternative be prepared for presentation at the May 18 meeting which had been scheduled for a final review of the program. This alternative, as prepared for presentation at the May 18 meeting, included the following basic changes from the vehicle described February 9:

1. Side glass replacing plastic side curtains.
2. Optional availability of an automatic transmission, power steering, power brakes, power windows, fender skirts, full wheel covers, and other standard car option and accessory items.
3. Seat changes abandoning the traditionally hard seats of European cars for added passenger comfort.
4. General interior restyling with the emphasis on luxury rather than function.
5. Suspension changes emphasizing passenger comfort instead of the ultimate in handling and cornering ability.

The financial data prepared for this alternative program indicated an increase in costs which would require 50 per cent higher sales volume than the true sports car to break even at a $3,500 list price. The alternative program, therefore, could only be profitable if substantially greater volume could be attained than the 10,000 estimated for a true sports car. This added volume would have to be attained in spite of the probable rejection of this vehicle by the followers of the true sports car.

II. EX-CELL-O CORPORATION

INTRODUCTION

SINCE its organization in 1919, Ex-Cell-O Corporation has expanded into a leading manufacturer of precision parts and assemblies, machine tools, cutting tools, and dairy equipment. Sales and operating revenues for 1957 were $168,877,000. Speaking at a meeting of the National Association of Investment Clubs, November 9, 1957, Mr. H. Glenn Bixby, president of Ex-Cell-O Corporation, stated: "While we have acquired a number of subsidiary companies, they all have one basic thing in common, the manufacture of precision metal products. In addition, the products of our subsidiary companies complement and supplement those of the parent company." In the company's annual report for 1957, Mr. Bixby further stated: "The record sales and operating revenues achieved in 1957 can be attributed to our policy of continually developing and acquiring new products to diversify further our sales volume." Exhibit I gives a percentage distribution of total sales and revenue dollars by major classes of products.

HISTORY

Ex-Cell-O was organized in 1919 by thirteen employees of the Ford Motor Company who invested their savings to form the Ex-Cell-O Tool and Manufacturing Company. The original plant consisted of only 2375 square feet of floor space located on the second floor of a small two-story building in downtown Detroit. The company's original products were drill jig bushings, tools, fixtures, and production parts for the automobile industry. From its inception, the philosophy of the company was "quality and precision on a mass-production basis."

By 1922, despite discouraging profits that year, the company had outgrown its original location. In a search for new capital, the Andreae family was induced to come to the company's rescue; two members of the family subsequently were elected to the Board of Directors.

Exhibit I

PERCENTAGE DISTRIBUTION OF TOTAL SALES AND REVENUE DOLLARS BY MAJOR CLASSES OF PRODUCTS OF EX-CELL-O CORPORATION*

Product Class	Percentage			
	1954	1955	1956	1957
Precision Parts and Assemblies	39.6	39.9	44.6	56.6
Dairy Equipment	25.5	27.3	19.4	18.7
Machine Tools and Accessories	28.7	23.7	28.3	18.3
Expendable Tools	6.2	9.1	7.7	6.4
	100.0	100.0	100.0	100.0

*SOURCE: *Annual Report*, November 30, 1955 and 1957.

The company moved into a leased building in 1923. The new quarters had floor space of 18,000 square feet. Soon afterward, the company developed its famous precision ball bearing which was later incorporated into the first models of Ex-Cell-O Precision Grinding Spindles. During the next five years, the company realized substantial production of precision parts and tool details for automobile, aircraft, and Diesel-engine manufacturers. Development of a precision boring machine was also undertaken.

Further expansion began in 1928, when the company built a modern plant of its own. This building provided 30,500 square feet of floor space, which was subsequently increased to 50,000 by an addition. The production volume of precision aircraft parts had become so important by 1929 that the company changed its name to "Ex-Cell-O Aircraft & Tool Corporation."

The following year, another building was erected to provide facilities for the new Machine Tool Division. Later that year, the company acquired one of the most modern tool shops in the country — Continental Tool Works. Continental's specialty was the manufacture of cutting tools for the metalworking industry. Prior to acquisition, Continental had been working closely with manufacturers of a new metal, tungsten carbide, which was second only to the diamond in hardness. In the fall of 1930, Ex-Cell-O was one of the first companies to announce that its cutting tools would be available with tungsten-carbide tips. Two years later, the company introduced the Ex-Cell-O Carbide Tool Grinder, first of its type, which was designed to condition carbide and other metal-cutting tools.

Expansion of facilities and experimental engineering continued during the 1930's. The company's main plant was enlarged and new machines were developed, such as the Ex-Cell-O Hydraulic Power Unit, the Precision Thread Grinder, the Center Lapping Machine, and the Ex-Cell-O Way-Type Precision Boring Machine.

The Pure-Pak Division was established in 1935, when Ex-Cell-O acquired from the American Paper Bottle Company of Toledo, Ohio, the rights to a paper milk container and the machinery to form, sterilize, fill, and seal it. This company had been working on this new method of marketing milk since the early 1920's. However, only a few machines had been put into operation. Ex-Cell-O manufactured and put into operation its first Pure-Pak machine late in 1936.

As a result of this widening product diversification, the company felt a need for a more inclusive corporate name. Hence, in 1937, its name was changed to "Ex-Cell-O Corporation," its present title.

In 1940, the company leased a plant on Hamilton Avenue, in Detroit, which contained over 100,000 square feet of floor space. Three later additions raised the total floor space to 544,000 square feet. Two years later, the main Oakman Plant was again enlarged. In addition, the company built and began operating for the government a new plant on Woodrow Wilson Avenue, containing 105,000 square feet. Total manufacturing space was almost a million square feet.

The volume of precision aircraft parts manufactured by the company during World War II was regarded as outstanding. Over 32 million parts were produced in 1942; 53 million in 1943. The total eventually reached 110 million parts produced in less than four years. For all Ex-Cell-O divisions, peak war production registered almost a 2000 per cent increase over the peacetime volume of 1938.

Considering the rapidly changing aviation industry, a very significant event took place in 1948 when the company acquired the Robbins Engineering Company, Detroit, an established supplier of jet-aircraft parts. This organization had specialized engineering, manufacturing, and testing facilities for producing compressor blades, rings, and complete rotor assemblies for jet-engine manufacturers.

New machines were developed by Ex-Cell-O for the production of jet details. Previous production methods for jet compressor blades had consisted of laborious hand machining. In 1951, the company developed the Ex-Cell-O Profile Milling Machine, the Precision Profile Grinder, the Blade Polishing Machine, and the Ex-Cell-O Two-Wheel Form Grinder, which simultaneously finish-grinds both sides of the blade root. The following year, the Vertical Precision Contouring Machine for turning the rings and wheels that carry the compressor blades was introduced.

More new machine tools were introduced into the company's standard line during the next few years. These included the Cam-Operated Precision Boring Machine, the Vertical Precision Boring Machine, the Scru-Broach, the Method X Tool Sharpener (electromechanical), and the Style 120 Thread Grinder.

Acquisitions and expansion continued. At year end, 1957, Ex-Cell-O Corporation (Consolidated) occupied 24 modern manufacturing plants located in the United States, Canada, and England. Total floor space exceeded two million square feet. Assets were $111,365,000; shareholders' equity was $72,288,000; total sales were $168,877,000; and net earnings after taxes were $14,054,000.

As an operating company, Ex-Cell-O had three manufacturing plants in Michigan, six in Ohio, one in Indiana, one in California, and one in North Carolina. In addition, it had an engineering and development department in Toledo, Ohio, and thirteen industrial sales offices strategically located throughout the United States. Each plant also had a sales office and sales staff. The company had a large number of independent sales representatives throughout the United States and in many foreign countries.

SUBSIDIARIES

Ex-Cell-O owned all outstanding stock of six operating domestic subsidiaries as follows:

The American Paper Bottle Company, acquired in 1944, functioned as a sales and service organization in Illinois for the Pure-Pak Division and operated a research and development engineering department for dairy equipment at Walled Lake, Michigan.

Robbins Engineering Company, acquired in 1948, manufactured jet-engine rotors and components in Detroit and operated a machine tool engineering department at Royal Oak, Michigan. Ex-Cell-O intended to discontinue Robbins' manufacturing operations and to expand its engineering functions.

Accurate Bushing Company, acquired in 1949, produced precision parts and drill jig bushings in Garwood, New Jersey.

Michigan Tool Company, another leading machine-tool company, was acquired in 1955. This subsidiary produced gear-making machines and tools, Roto-Flo spline rolling machines and tools, and automation equipment at Detroit and Manistee, Michigan, and Cone Drive speed reducers and gearsets at Traverse City, Michigan.

The Smith Bearing Company, acquired in 1957, manufactured needle bearings primarily for the aircraft industry and cam follower bearings at Trenton, New Jersey.

Cadillac Gage Company, acquired in 1956, had plants in Roseville, Michigan, and Costa Mesa, California. Cadillac manufactured various types of gauges, fire-control equipment for tanks, and servo-valve mechanisms for aircraft and missiles.

Ex-Cell-O also had three foreign subsidiaries. Ex-Cello-O Corporation of Canada, Ltd., organized in 1953, produced machine tools, railroad pins and bushings, drill jig bushings and precision parts in London, Canada. Ex-Cell-O Corporation (Machine Tools), Ltd., of Lancaster, England, began manufacturing machine tools and accessories in 1954. Colonial Tool Company, Ltd., was acquired in 1955 along with Michigan Tool Company. Colonial produced broaches and cutting tools in Windsor and Montreal, Canada.

In speaking before the National Association of Investment Clubs, November 9, 1957, H. Glenn Bixby, Ex-Cell-O's president, stated: "We are interested in strengthening our earning power and diversifying our product line. If this can be accomplished in the future through the acquisition of subsidiary companies on a proper basis, we are certainly not averse to such acquisitions. We do not acquire companies merely to get large or appear aggressive."

MACHINE TOOLS AND ACCESSORIES

Ex-Cell-O's machine-tool classification consisted of a large variety of types and models which ranged from relatively small, simple center lapping machines, carbide tool grinders, high-speed precision internal grinders, internal and external precision thread grinders, precision boring machines, jet blade milling, grinding and polishing machines, to huge special purpose machinery and complex automated machinery and devices which provided for continuous classification and flow of parts between successive assembly-line stages. Vertical gear shaving machines, Roto-Flo spline rollers, ultra speed gear hobbers, Shear Speed gear shapers and involute gear checkers were manufactured by a subsidiary, Michigan Tool Company.

The company also produced many important machine-tool accessories, such as precision spindles and hydraulic power units. Precision spindles were first introduced by Ex-Cell-O in 1923 and have since been constantly under development and improvement. Having sold over 100,000 units to date, the company is regarded as one of the largest, if not the largest, manufacturers of precision ball-bearing spindles in the world. As a result of their combined accuracy and rigidity, Ex-Cell-O spindles received world-wide recognition for their performance and dependability. Hydraulic power units are another important machine-tool accessory. These are self-contained, compact power units designed for actuating single tools or multiple spindle heads for drilling, reaming, counterboring, spot facing, and other similar machining operations. The company incorporates such units in many of its own special machine tools. They are also used extensively on machine tools manufactured by many other leading companies.

PRECISION PARTS AND ASSEMBLIES

The Parts Division manufactures a wide range of precision products for the aircraft, railroad, farm equipment, construction, and many other industries.

Products for the aircraft industry include electrical and hydraulic actuators, fuel metering devices, spray bars and nozzles. Because of the highly precise nature of these assemblies, Ex-Cell-O's development and design engineering departments worked very closely with aircraft customers. Other aircraft products included blades and wheels used in jet-aircraft engines.

Pins and bushing which were used in spring and brake rigging of both locomotives and cars were manufactured for the railroad industry.

Michigan Tool Company's Cone Drive speed reducer units and gearsets had a wide variety of applications in paper mills, steel mills, chemical plants, and other industries.

Many other parts were manufactured which had wide commercial application; these included worm gears, lead screws, sleeves, guide rollers, and liners.

EXPENDABLE TOOLS

Even though the dollar volume of sales for this line of products has been small relative to other product lines, the company has considered this line important because it includes perishable tools from which the company obtains considerable repeat business.

This division manufactures a complete line of special cutting tools used with machine tools, and includes counterbores, face mills, milling cutters, broaches, carbide-tipped tools, reamers and gear hobbers, shavers, and cutters. In addition, a complete line of drill jig bushings is manufactured; such bushings are used throughout the metalworking industry.

DAIRY EQUIPMENT

The Pure-Pak Division manufactures milk-packaging machines which are leased or sold to the dairy industry. These machines automatically form, sterilize, fill, and seal paper cartons of milk on a volume production basis.

From 1936 to 1945 the company manufactured and installed approximately 160 machines; as of 1957, over 3000 machines were in operation. In 1937, 42 thousand Pure-Pak containers were used; over 9 billion were used in 1957.

The early machines packaged only half-pint, pint, and quart size containers. The first half-gallon machine was introduced in the Los Angeles market in 1940. In 1957, almost 2½ billion half-gallon containers were used.

Approximately 65 per cent of all milk packaged in paper in

the United States in 1957 was packaged in Pure-Pak containers; over one third of all bottled milk (paper and glass) was Pure-Pak.

Since the company was primarily in the machine-tool business, it did not manufacture the paper containers, but instead licensed paper companies (carton converters) to manufacture and sell blank cartons to the dairies. Ex-Cell-O did, however, manufacture and sell the machinery for producing blanks to carton converters.

Wax, wire, and glue were available to the dairies through a large number of suppliers. Ex-Cell-O acted as sales representatives for a few of these suppliers.

The Pure-Pak market consisted of the United States, Canada, South America, and various countries in Europe and Asia. About 185 machines were in operation in foreign countries. A number of agencies acted as foreign representatives.

One of the obstacles to greater use of Pure-Pak in Europe had been the cost of transporting blanks from the United States. Recently, however, Ex-Cell-O licensed carton-converting companies in Norway, Denmark, and Belgium.

There are six standard models of Pure-Pak machines, as well as various other dairy equipment. Exhibit II shows these standard models and the number of cartons packaged per minute.

The machines were either leased or sold to the dairy industry. As an example, for a Senior Quart machine the lease consisted of a $2,850 down payment, followed by 60 consecutive monthly base rentals of $485, for a total of $31,950. In addition, monthly production rentals were paid during the life of the machine. The latter rentals were based on a millage for the number of cartons sold per month by the dairy; the rate varied according to size of carton. Production rental discounts were offered, with higher discounts for higher volumes of production. As compared to these basic lease costs, the Senior Quart machine would cost $100,000, if purchased outright. It was generally believed that the leasing arrangement had enabled many financially limited dairies to acquire Pure-Pak machines. Approximately 95 per cent of all Pure-Pak machines had been leased.

The company employed 96 resident engineers to service Pure-Pak equipment in the United States and Canada. Each man was responsible for about 30 machines in his territory; he maintained constant inspection and serviced machines when necessary. Parts

Exhibit II

STANDARD PURE-PAK MACHINES AND
RELATED PRODUCTION

Model	Cartons Packaged per minute
Midget Quart (½ pt., pt., qt.)	20
Junior Quart (½ pt., pt., qt.)	45
Senior Quart (½ pt., pt., qt.)	75
Midget Half-Gallon	16
Junior Half-Gallon	33
Senior Half-Gallon	50

depots were located in several areas in the United States for immediate shipment of repair parts.

Since the wholesale market had approached saturation, being dominated by Pure-Pak packaged milk, the company was planning to concentrate future sales effort toward converting retail routes to Pure-Pak. This was to be accomplished by making the consumer and milkman more conscious of the advantages Pure-Pak offered, and thus increasing the number of dairies that were "standardized" (100 per cent) Pure-Pak operations.

SALES

The company's sales force consisted of two main classifications: Pure-Pak Sales and Industrial Sales. Pure-Pak sales were handled by 20 men, each having a territory in the United States and Canada. Agents and independent representatives handled foreign dairy sales.

Industrial products were sold through company branch offices, the home office, manufacturers' agents, and export agents. Branch salesmen generally sold all industrial products throughout their territories. However, large accounts were often serviced by specialized salesmen from the home office, or under its direct supervision. Salesmen were paid a base salary plus commissions.

The company was gradually expanding and consolidating branch office forces to serve its customers better and, in addition, to avoid duplication of branch facilities involving both parent and subsidiary sales offices.

ACCOUNTING

Ex-Cell-O used a Job-Cost accounting system. The actual time spent and pieces produced at a particular operation were recorded by the worker on labor tickets which were summarized weekly by tabulating machines. Material was also charged to individual jobs, whenever possible, through the use of material requisitions. The company's Estimating Department compared these actual costs against their estimates.

Comparative financial data for selected years is given in Exhibits III and IV.

THE FUTURE

The following account of the company's future potential growth, assuming a relatively stable economic climate, is condensed from Mr. Bixby's speech before the National Association of Investment Clubs, November 9, 1957.

Growth potential for Ex-Cell-O's Machine Tool and Expendable Tool Divisions would probably result from two causes. First, the industry was finding competition keener and selling price of great importance. The installation of modern machine tools that gave high volume output at low unit cost was one of the best means of keeping costs down. Ex-Cell-O was constantly improving its standard machine tools and developing special new equipment designed for high volume output at low unit cost. The second potential for growth in the company's Machine Tool Division was industry's demand for automated equipment. Because of current high labor costs and the probability of even higher costs in the future, Mr. Bixby believed that industry would obviously search for labor-saving equipment to keep manufacturing costs in line; increased costs could not be continually passed on to consumers without causing reduced demand. Ex-Cell-O had long experience in automation relative to its individual machine tools and to its fully automated production lines of equipment.

In regard to precision parts and assemblies, Mr. Bixby pointed out the company's history as a major producer of parts for piston-type aircraft engines and its transition to jet-engine components. Currently, the company's largest volume of business in its Pre-

EX-CELL-O CORPORATION

Exhibit III

COMPARATIVE BALANCE SHEETS AS OF DECEMBER 31, 1939–1943, AND NOVEMBER 30, 1946–1957* (In Thousands)

ASSETS	1939	1943	1946	1949	1952	1953	1954	1955	1956	1957
Current Assets:										
Cash	$ 328	$ 4,272	$ 1,486	$ 2,751	$ 6,619	$ 6,395	$ 4,350	$ 4,272	$ 10,999	$ 9,115
Marketable Securities			95	7						9,000
Receivables (Net)	987	6,050	2,928	4,215	10,398	9,433	8,631	9,548	19,743	13,752
Inventory (Lower of Cost or Market)	1,222	8,556	5,182	4,820	15,314	18,806	15,249	22,301	34,798	31,149
Total Current Assets	$2,537	$18,878	$ 9,691	$11,793	$32,331	$34,634	$28,230	$36,121	$ 65,540	$ 63,016
Investments	$ 21	$ 198	$ 1,070	$ 3,770			$ 1,380	$ 1,667	$ 1,713	$ 158
Receivables With Extended Maturities	1,837	2,859	5,139	5,291	$ 8,703	$ 9,441	9,936	12,891	18,169	22,862
Net Plant, Equipment, and Tools	721	588	3,671	9,648	13,430	14,697	16,957	17,025	19,444	22,140
Rental Machinery (Net)		378								
Due From Government on Emergency Facilities										
Patents	67	548	589	1,295	955	864	802	778	1,621	1,599
Prepaid Expense and Deferred Charges			260	665	543	512	648	858	884	1,027
Goodwill Less Amortization										563
Total Assets	$5,183	$23,449	$20,420	$32,462	$55,962	$60,148	$57,953	$69,340	$107,371	$111,365
LIABILITIES AND CAPITAL										
Current Liabilities:										
Accounts and Notes Payable	$ 551	$ 1,138	$ 571	$ 2,516†	$ 6,041	$ 7,539	$ 4,294	$ 7,507	$ 14,363	$ 12,055
Taxes (Federal, State, Social Security)	261	7,852**	1,875	2,598	8,124	8,806	5,407	3,719	14,006	12,007
Customers' Deposits	387	1,673	364	94	1,355	270		364	530	359
Other Accounts and Dividends Payable††	100	2,232	553	277	351	386	850	882	907	1,361
Total Current Liabilities	$1,299	$12,895	$ 3,363	$ 5,485	$15,871	$17,001	$11,045	$12,472	$ 29,806	$ 25,782
Fixed Liabilities:										
Loans	$ 21	$ 50	$ 3,000	$ 1,500	$ 9,875	$ 7,750	$ 4,500	$ 3,500	$ 13,500	$ 10,500
Insurance Reserve			50	50	50	50				
Contingency Reserve		600	100	100	100	600	650	650	650	
Deferred Rental Income	285	379	1,618	7,246	2,169	2,360	2,617	2,508	2,611	2,795
Bonus to Executives (Stock)	22									
Total Fixed Liabilities	$ 328	$ 1,029	$ 4,768	$ 8,896	$12,194	$10,760	$ 7,767	$ 6,658	$ 16,761	$ 13,295
Total Liabilities	$1,627	$13,924	$ 8,131	$14,381	$28,065	$27,761	$18,812	$19,130	$ 46,567	$ 39,077
Capital and Surplus:										
Stock Issued	$1,184	$ 1,196	$ 1,196	$ 1,277	$ 2,108	$ 2,318	$ 2,550	$ 5,370	$ 5,370	$ 10,890
Capital Surplus	720	773	773	1,664	10,366	13,246	16,876	21,241	21,241	21,837
Earned Surplus	1,652	7,556	10,320	15,140	15,423	16,823	19,715	23,456	34,050	37,668
Less Treasury Stock at Cost								(1,250)	(1,250)	
Stock Held by Escrow Agent										(500)
Excess of Equity in Subsidiary								1,393	1,393	1,393
Total Capital and Surplus	$3,556	$ 9,525	$12,289	$18,081	$27,897	$32,387	$39,141	$50,210	$ 60,804	$ 72,288
Total Liabilities and Capital	$5,183	$23,449	$20,420	$32,462	$55,962	$60,148	$57,953	$69,340	$107,371	$111,365

*Source: Company annual reports.
**After $13,021,000 tax notes.

†Includes item reported under "Other Accounts Payable" in prior years.
††Payroll and commercial only, 1936–1941 inclusive: Dividends only 1949.

Exhibit IV

EX-CELL-O CORPORATION

COMPARATIVE OPERATING STATEMENTS ENDING DECEMBER 31, 1939, AND NOVEMBER 30, 1943–1957* (In Thousands)

	1939	1943	1946	1949	1952	1953	1954	1955	1956	1957
Sales (Net)	$6,608	$63,881	$18,306	$25,577	$76,912	$84,164	$76,488	$74,632	$130,749	$147,373
Rents and Royalties on Leased and Licensed Equipment	.....	975	996	5,973	12,064	13,341	15,790	17,843	19,508	21,504
Gross Income	$6,608	$64,856	$19,302	$31,550	$88,976	$97,505	$92,278	$92,475	$150,257	$168,877
Cost of Sales and Leased and Licensed Equipment	4,656	51,860	15,634	22,790	64,024	70,061	67,149	67,217	111,070	128,616
Gross Profit	$1,962	$12,996	$ 3,668	$ 8,760	$24,952	$27,444	$25,129	$25,258	$ 39,187	$ 40,261
Selling Expense	$ 782	$ 2,683	$ 2,034	$ 2,325	$ 4,172	$ 4,826	$ 4,493	$ 5,423	$ 7,559	$ 7,923
Administrative and General Expense	152	1,069	480	806	1,362	1,442	1,636	2,253	2,609	3,080
Total Expenses	$ 934	$ 3,752	$ 2,514	$ 3,131	$ 5,534	$ 6,268	$ 6,129	$ 7,676	$ 10,168	$ 11,003
Operating Profit	$1,018	$ 9,244	$ 1,154	$ 5,629	$19,418	$21,176	$19,000	$17,582	$ 29,019	$ 29,258
Other Income (Net of Other Charges)	36	260	645	112	174	(187)	303	999	603	337
Total	$1,054	$ 9,504	$ 1,799	$ 5,741	$19,592	$20,989	$19,303	$18,581	$ 29,622	$ 29,595
Other Charges (Interest)	2	45	15	57	427	352	278	189	373	691
Profit Before Taxes	$1,052	$ 9,459	$ 1,784	$ 5,684	$19,165	$20,637	$19,025	$18,392	$ 29,249	$ 28,904
U. S. and Foreign Income Taxes	180	6,829	574	2,165	13,427	14,637	10,185	9,450	15,100	14,850
Net Profit	$ 872	$ 2,630	$ 1,210	$ 3,519	$ 5,738	$ 6,000	$ 8,840	$ 8,942	$ 14,149	$ 14,054
Special Items	.....	300	.....	.....	.....	.....	.....	600**	.....	.....
Net Profit to Surplus	$ 872	$ 2,330	$ 1,210	$ 3,519	$ 5,738	$ 6,000	$ 8,840	$ 9,542	$ 14,149	$ 14,054

*Sources: Company annual reports.
**Recovery of federal taxes, based principally on World War II relief claims, $844,572, less provision for net renegotiation adjustments, fiscal year 1952, $245,000.

cision Products Division was for jet engines used almost exclusively by the military. Ex-Cell-O anticipated a lessening in this demand in the next few years, but believed this reduction would be offset somewhat by civilian demand for commercial jet transports such as the Douglas DC8 and the Boeing 707. Orders were on hand for over 400 jet transports — constituting a demand for almost 2000 jet engines. Since Ex-Cell-O was currently supplying parts and assemblies for the two manufacturers who would supply these engines, Pratt & Whitney and General Electric, the company expected the demand for its related components to continue for some time.

Mr. Bixby pointed out the company's awareness of the impending transition from jet to rocket engines. It was noted that the rocket-engine industry's sales in 1957 were approximately 450 million dollars, would reach one billion dollars by 1960, and would continue to increase. Although rocket engines contained fewer machined parts than jet engines, there still was a need for highly precisioned parts for valving, turbo pumps, high temperature servo valves, actuators and inertial guidance systems. Ex-Cell-O expected to get its share of rocket-engine business and to make the transition from jet engines to rocket engines as it did from piston to jet engines.

Concerning the growth potential for Ex-Cell-O's Pure-Pak Dairy Division, Mr. Bixby pointed out the major change in the method of packaging milk during the previous twenty years. In 1940, less than 5 per cent of all bottled milk was packaged in paper containers; by 1950, 31 per cent; by 1954, 50.6 per cent. The company estimated that paper containers would account for almost 60 per cent of all milk bottled in the United States by the end of 1957. It was believed this growth indicated a revolutionary change in packaging milk and showed a definite consumer preference for lightweight, safe, and disposable paper milk containers such as Pure-Pak.

Mr. Bixby believed the increased use of Pure-Pak cartons had been even more remarkable than the total increased use of paper cartons. Since its introduction in 1936, Pure-Pak carton sales increased from less than 200 million cartons in 1940 to over 9 billion cartons in 1956; sales for 1958 might reach 10 billion cartons.

There has been a significant shift within the company's own container sales resulting in a definite preference for half-gallon cartons over quart-size cartons. Beginning in 1949, the company experienced a rapid rise in half-gallon container sales. By the end of 1955, the amount of milk sold in Pure-Pak half-gallon containers exceeded the amount sold in Pure-Pak quart containers. The use of half-gallon containers increased 29.3 per cent between 1955 and 1956. An additional increase of 21 per cent was expected in 1957. This indicated a definite consumer preference for the large economy sized half-gallon carton. Since Pure-Pak had the only half-gallon carton in the industry, the company believed this preference was a decided advantage to Pure-Pak's future growth potential.

The company also recognized the potential demand for its container in the foreign market. As of 1957, Pure-Pak equipment had been installed in twenty-four foreign countries. Because of different economic conditions, however, Ex-Cell-O did not expect as spectacular success in the foreign market as was experienced in the domestic market.

The ultimate aim of the company was to have the dairy industry standardize on the Pure-Pak container. An increasing number of dairies were finding it uneconomical to have a dual operation of both paper and glass. Because of this, the company was aggressive in its attempts to have its customers convert to 100 per cent Pure-Pak operations. By 1957, more than 400 dairies had standardized on Pure-Pak. Ex-Cell-O believed that as the cost of dual operations increased, more and more dairies would convert their entire operations to Pure-Pak.

III. AMERICAN LUMBER COMPANY

THE American Lumber Company is a commercial and industrial supplier located in Detroit, Michigan. Its operations are conducted in three basic areas. The first is a manufacturing plant which currently employs eight men. Here the company manufactures wooden boxes, crates, and pallets for various industrial accounts located in the Detroit area. The second area is that of general lumber sales. Here lumber purchased from mills in various parts of the United States and Canada are distributed to commercial building contractors and industrial accounts. The third area, the newest to the company, is that of a millwork supplier. This consists in competitive bidding for such items as doors, cabinets, and paneling in commercial and industrial buildings. Any retail business with the general public is negligible in size and undesired by the company. Sales for the company had averaged approximately $500,000 in recent years. No attempt had been made to determine accurately how much of the sales had been generated from any of the basic areas.

The company was founded in 1933 by William R. Reade as a retail lumberyard catering to house builders. Operations were conducted successfully until 1941. At that time, Mr. Reade, who was independently wealthy, had grown tired of the increasing complexities of the business. The Office of Price Administration had instituted its wartime regulations, and rationing had been instituted in the industry. Mr. Reade felt that these, together with the limitations placed upon house building, made the profit potential simply not worth the effort. Accordingly, the company ceased operations in early 1942.

In 1944, Mr. Reade was approached by Mr. Philip Smith, a former customer, with a business proposition. Mr. Smith, who had built houses prior to the war, now was engaged in manufacturing wooden boxes and crates for industrial companies in war work. He was, however, hampered in two respects. First of all, he lacked sufficient working capital to carry on the business. Second, the lumber mills were reluctant to handle orders from

111

new accounts. In general, they preferred to sell the limited supply only to their established customers. Mr. Smith felt that Mr. Reade could supply the additional capital and also receive favorable consideration from the mills. Mr. Reade agreed that the proposition offered good possibilities and resumed his company's operations. Mr. Smith became the secretary and treasurer of the company. Controlling interest was retained by Mr. Reade.

Until the end of the war in 1945, the operations of the company were limited to the box business. However, with the end of the wartime controls in the industry, a regular lumber trade was gradually started.

In 1948, Mr. Reade died, leaving his interest in the business to his wife. Under a prior agreement, this interest was sold to Mr. Smith under the terms of a personal note and a long-term land contract on the property.

The company was reorganized with Mr. Smith becoming president and his wife vice-president. The company attorney assumed the office of secretary while the company insurance man became treasurer. These men had been close personal friends of both Mr. Reade and Mr. Smith. Both held only the legal minimum number of stock shares and were inactive in the direction of the business.

The death of Mr. Reade brought one major change in policy as the repurchase of his stock limited the working capital of the company. As a result, Mr. Smith decided to redirect the sales effort. Instead of returning to supplying house builders, he decided to concentrate efforts toward the commercial contractors. His reasoning was that it was traditional for house builders to require extensive credit whereas the commercial contractors normally handled their obligations in thirty days.

Duties in the company were apportioned in the following manner. Mr. Smith supervised the financial aspects, handled the office routine with the aid of a bookkeeper, did the carload purchasing, and made the sales to the general contractors. Herbert Jones was employed as superintendent of the company. He directed the box manufacturing and the shipment of the lumber. In addition, he handled the purchasing from various local wholesalers. Mr. Smith considered him a man of exceptional ability. He had been with the company since its inception in 1934. Prior to this, he had been employed as a foreman in various wood-working plants in Detroit and possessed considerable skill in operating this type of equipment. One salesman was employed to solicit the box and industrial lumber sales.

In late 1953, Mr. Smith brought his son-in-law, Robert Kelly, into the business. Mr. Kelly, a graduate engineer, had just completed Korean War service as a naval officer. He was to relieve Mr. Smith of the general contractor sales and to develop the millwork phase that Mr. Smith had started. His initial efforts in the area made it seem that it offered good possibilities. Within three months, however, the industrial salesman resigned to form his own company. Consequently, Mr. Kelly was shifted to this area and was able to continue calling on only a few general contractors.

In 1955, Mr. Smith brought another son-in-law, Mr. James Sweeney, into the company. He had had several years of college and a brief amount of experience at another lumberyard. His duties were to contact general contractors for the lumber and millwork business. Mr. Smith felt that this type business could be handled without any additional employees and with the existing facilities.

In 1959, Mr. Smith was confronted with serious difficulties. Sales had varied widely in the past nine years. While the general trend was slightly upward, profits had slid considerably. In fact, slight losses had been incurred in two of the past three years. In general, he felt it was time for a reassessment of the company policies. There had been gradual changes in every area in which the company worked. The box plant had been organized by the Teamsters Union in 1948 and wages had skyrocketed. Whereas they had been an average of $1.60 in 1950, the average rate had now risen to $2.15 per hour. What complicated the situation further was that the majority of the competition was located outside the Detroit area and had not been organized by the union. As a result, their average wage was in the neighborhood of $1.25 per hour. This differential had been offset to a degree by soliciting "short runs" of boxes where the transportation costs of the competition balanced the higher wages. Then, too, there were certain accounts which required rapid delivery that could not be satisfied outside the Detroit area. Competition was drawing these markets tighter. More of the low-volume orders were being solicited by the out-of-town competitors. Even the accounts that had required rapid delivery were improving their scheduling procedures to take advantage of the lower prices.

One factor that concerned Mr. Smith was the lack of a cost system in the company. Several years earlier he had attempted to initiate a system, but Herb Jones, the superintendent, had refused to put it into effect. He had stated that the runs were too small to obtain accurate figures. Furthermore, he stated that too much time would be wasted in keeping the necessary records. The matter had ended with that. Mr. Smith revived the idea in late 1958, but was rebuffed in the same fashion. Thus, labor figures continued to be estimated by Mr. Jones on new jobs on the basis of his experience.

Mr. Kelly suggested the possibility that air-driven automatic hand nailers might be installed to replace the present hand-nailing system. His preliminary investigation had shown that an expenditure of approximately two thousand dollars would be required to install the system. Mr. Jones had protested violently that the project was unworkable. The cost, in his opinion, made it uneconomical. He also argued that it would require hiring a mechanic to keep it in working order. To the best of Mr. Kelly's knowledge, Mr. Jones was not at all familiar with the machinery. In any event, because of Mr. Jones' objections, Mr. Smith lost interest in the project.

In the area of lumber sales, competition was also keen. The majority of the companies vying for the general contractors' business was substantially larger than the American Lumber Co. Accordingly, Mr. Smith estimated that they were able to purchase in larger volumes for a price approximately 1 per cent lower than he could obtain. Since the gross mark-up was approximately 12 per cent on lumber, it made a substantial difference. Until the present, the policy of the company had been to sell on a service basis rather than price. This was becoming extremely difficult since the competition among general contractors had also grown more stiff. In more and more instances, any price differential was being seized upon. Mr. Smith felt that more intensive sales was necessary.

Millwork was also suffering from competition, though it did

Exhibit I

AMERICAN LUMBER COMPANY
COMPARATIVE BALANCE SHEET, DECEMBER 31, 1950–1958

ASSETS	1950	1951	1952	1953
Current Assets:				
Cash	$ 5,723	$ 15,667	$ 720	$ 3,572
Accounts Receivable	34,000	36,666	56,309	58,410
Inventory	29,895	36,990	36,375	36,471
Total Current Assets	$ 70,527	$ 89,323	$ 93,404	$ 98,453
Property, Equipment, Plant (Less Reserve)	5,870	8,027	37,952	34,324
Deferred Charges	518	1,622	1,308	1,522
Other Assets	1,223	2,162	10,540	11,205
Total Assets	$ 78,138	$101,134	$142,652	$145,504
LIABILITIES AND CAPITAL				
Current Liabilities	$ 15,756	$ 24,634	$ 22,566	$ 23,654
Long-Term Debt			35,961	25,955
Capital Stock	50,000	50,000	50,000	50,000
Earned Surplus	12,382	26,491	34,677	45,895
Total Liabilities and Capital	$ 78,138	$101,134	$142,652	$145,504

ASSETS	1954	1955	1956	1957	1958
Current Assets:					
Cash	$ 2,542	$ 12,876	$ 8,368	$ 14,974	$ 2,247
Accounts Receivable	69,003	64,015	55,088	80,270	53,738
Inventory	35,223	28,633	33,981	26,748	38,628
Total Current Assets	$105,768	$105,524	$ 93,437	$121,990	$ 94,613
Property, Equipment, Plant (Less Reserve)	31,677	33,080	34,678	30,830	32,878
Deferred Charges	2,440	2,786	2,260	1,632	2,058
Other Assets	1,767	2,383	3,033	3,125	5,810
Total Assets	$142,652	$143,773	$137,408	$157,577	$135,368
LIABILITIES AND CAPITAL					
Current Liabilities	$ 29,875	$ 30,217	$ 28,274	$ 51,213	$ 35,117
Long-Term Debt	18,652	14,674	10,424	6,101	1,551
Capital Stock	50,000	50,000	50,000	50,000	50,000
Earned Surplus	44,149	48,882	48,710	50,263	48,700
Total Liabilities and Capital	$142,652	$143,773	$137,408	$157,577	$135,368

not appear to be as severe as in other areas. American was hampered from maximizing profits in this area by several factors. Many of the contracts involved as much as 40 per cent cabinetwork. Since American did not have a cabinet shop, it was necessary to subcontract this phase. Consequently, only a small mark-up could be obtained on this part of the contracts. The same situation existed in the special moldings and panelings that were sometimes required. In general, however, the company felt that a satisfactory profit was obtained on these contracts. Yet, no

Exhibit II

AMERICAN LUMBER COMPANY
CONSOLIDATED INCOME STATEMENT
FOR THE YEARS ENDED 1950–1958

	1950	1951	1952	1953	
Net Sales	$348,550	$517,320	$484,996	$536,119	
Cost of Sales	306,463	454,125	429,680	475,667	
Gross Margin	$ 42,087	$ 63,195	$ 55,316	$ 60,452	
Selling, General, and Administrative Expenses	35,085	42,631	41,280	44,288	
Profit From Operation	$ 7,002	$ 20,564	$ 14,036	$ 16,164	
Other Income	59	63	23	43	
Other Deductions	1,734	669	1,939	2,938	
Net Profit Before Taxes	$ 5,327	$ 19,958	$ 12,120	$ 13,269	
Income Taxes	1,302	5,851	3,930	4,050	
Net Profit After Taxes	$ 4,025	$ 14,107	$ 8,190	$ 9,219	
	1954	1955	1956	1957	1958
Net Sales	$425,616	$531,115	$484,579	$570,231	$452,620
Cost of Sales	381,181	474,993	440,702	514,819	405,492
Gross Margin	$ 44,435	$ 56,122	$ 44,877	$ 55,412	$ 47,128
Selling, General, and Administrative Expenses	40,684	46,811	42,362	51,548	48,217
Profit From Operation	$ 3,751	$ 9,311	$ 2,515	$ 3,864	$ (1,089)
Other Income	10	33	198	283	932
Other Deductions	3,255	2,460	2,739	1,744	2,494
Net Profit Before Taxes	$ 506	$ 6,884	$ (16)	$ 2,403	$ (1,562)
Income Taxes	254	2,151	157	852	...
Net Profit After Taxes	$ 252	$ 4,733	$ (173)	$ 1,551	$ (1,562)

cost records were kept on the jobs to substantiate this feeling. The foregoing was, in general, the situation confronting Mr. Smith. He was reluctant to consider dropping any of the operations. He felt that there was distinct advantage in the widely separated areas. The industrial box and lumber sales normally were at their peak during the fall and winter months tapering off in the spring. In contrast, the construction lumber and millwork reached their peaks in the spring and summer. This produced a desirable balance with an even level of use of the capacity of the company.

With regard to the financial aspects of the company, Mr. Smith felt that there was a general weakening in its status. Exhibits I and II give the balance sheets and income statements for recent dates and periods of operation.

IV. McLOUTH STEEL CORPORATION

THE McLouth Steel Corporation was founded in 1934 to process semifinished slabs into hot rolled strips, primarily for the automobile industry. The basic equipment was a single stand reversing rolling mill of a type not used before in the United States steel industry. It cost approximately $350,000 and could operate comparatively cheaply, but only after great toil and ingenuity. The company had no steelmaking facilities, but bought semifinished slabs and rolled them into a finished hot rolled strip. A cold mill was added in 1938 and in 1945 stainless steel was added to the product mix. These minor expansions were financed by debt and were quickly repaid from retained earnings and provided the basis for two much larger programs in 1948 and 1953.

In 1947 McLouth was informed by its supplier of semifinished steel that it would have to look for another source as its supplier required all of its semifinished steel for its own mills. Since this was at the time of a steel shortage, the corporation could not obtain another supplier. It was a question of making its own steel or getting out of business. At this time its plant investment was $2,800,000; long-term debt, $350,000; and net profit for 1947, $1,700,000. McLouth needed $22,500,000 to buy four electric furnaces that would produce nearly 600,000 tons a year and make it the only steel company using electric furnaces exclusively for carbon as well as stainless steel.[1] Since the automotive industry wanted to keep McLouth in business, General Motors loaned $4,000,000; Ford Motor Company $2,000,000; Briggs Manufacturing Company and American Metal Products $1,000,000 each. The reconstruction Finance Corporation put up the remaining $14,500,000.

The electric furnaces were installed at a new mill in Trenton, Michigan. The making of steel in an electric furnace requires 1.07 tons of scrap for every ton produced. Since the price of scrap fluctuates widely, this placed McLouth in a weak competitive

---

[1] Stainless steel was not melted in the electrics in 1947.

position compared with fully integrated companies. The late Donald B. McLouth, founder and president at that time, decided to integrate the company more fully. To achieve this, he needed two large electric furnaces, a new blast furnace, a new steelmaking plant that would include a continuous cold mill in Gibraltar, Michigan, and improvements to existing facilities. This would require $105,000,000, but his total capitalization was only $32,000,000 and his working capital $7,500,000.

A financial plan of this undertaking appeared to be staggering, but financiers considered McLouth an excellent credit risk because it had a long record of regular debt payments. McLouth has long been a pioneer among steel companies. Its explorations into new financing systems and production methods have been motivated more by necessity than by choice. Always cash hungry and debt ridden, McLouth has had to go through many corporate contortions to stay alive and healthy. These contortions have frequently landed it out in front in some phase of steelmaking. Included in the expansion program were plans for the first oxygen converters to make steel in the United States.

Since McLouth is located in the automotive industries back yards and the bulk of its production ended up on wheels, the automobile industry, as before, would do all it could to help. To the automobile manufacturers, the presence of steelmakers in Detroit means delivery within hours on rush orders. Moreover, McLouth and other Detroit mills enjoy a cost advantage because steel companies absorb some of the transportation costs. A Detroit automaker pays roughly the same for a ton of steel from Detroit or Pittsburgh leaving a better margin for their Detroit producer.

McLouth held a strong position in the stainless-steel market. About 73 per cent of its stainless production goes to the automobile industry which also takes about 80 per cent of its carbon-steel production. Stainless-steel accounts for about 7 per cent of McLouth's net tonnage production and because stainless steel sells for far more than carbon steel, stainless accounts for about 32 per cent of gross income. In addition, General Motors agreed to buy at least 5 per cent of its annual steel requirements from McLouth.

The capital to integrate the company more fully and increase its capacity to approximately 1,500,000 net tons of steel ingots, was obtained as follows: $14,000,000 of secured bank notes from a group of bankers headed by the National Bank of Detroit; $56,000,000 of first mortgage bonds due in 1972; $8,000,000 from income notes due in 1982 to the Metropolitan Life Insurance Company and the Prudential Insurance Company; and $25,000,000 and $2,000,000 of participating preferred stock to General Motors Corporation and American Metal Production Company respectively. The bank notes were issued at $3\frac{1}{4}$ per cent, the first mortgage bonds $4\frac{1}{4}$ per cent, the income notes $5\frac{1}{4}$ per cent, and the preferred stock at $5\frac{1}{4}$ per cent.

The capitalization ratios as of December 31, 1955, were fixed debt, 45.7 per cent; income debt and preferred stock, 24.8 per cent; and common stock and surplus, 29.5 per cent. Sales and net profits had increased from $17,000,000 and $1,700,000 in 1947 to $164,000,000 and $9,000,000 in 1956. Figures available for 1957 showed a substantial increase in view of an industry-wide decline. The corporations gross property, plant, and equipment of $139,-567,298 at April 30, 1957, included $136,655,016 or 97.9 per cent for net additions made since January 1, 1948.

The corporation sells its carbon steel primarily in the Detroit area where it does not have to equalize freight. It maintains district sales offices in Chicago, Indianapolis, Cincinnati, and Philadelphia. Nonautomotive-type stainless steel is sold nationally through a nationwide network of independent steel warehouses, jobbers, and distributors.

V. LAKE ERIE ASPHALT PAVING CORPORATION

HISTORY

In 1928, Mr. Daniel Swartz purchased controlling stock in the Lake Erie Cement Co. The company was selling asphaltic cements to industrial companies for maintaining their factory floors. Sales of asphaltic materials were also made to contractors for waterproofing jobs.

In 1936, Mr. Swartz expanded his company to the extent that he was not only selling asphaltic materials, but installing them as well. This expansion of the company brought up two of his brothers, Ron and Ken, from Ohio. They were made foremen of the mastic and waterproofing jobs.

In 1940, Daniel Swartz made another change — he was now paving driveways and parking lots. He purchased the materials from Chrysler Asphalt Paving and Alexander Asphalt Paving Companies. These companies had their own asphalt plants and occasionally sold materials to small independent contractors.

In 1946, Chrysler Asphalt Paving and the Alexander Asphalt Paving Companies acquired contracts with the city of Detroit which required them to work at night only. The traffic problem on the city streets during the daytime prevented profitable working time, so night work was the only answer. This action cut off the asphaltic-material source of supply to the independent contractors, and just at the time when Lake Erie Asphalt Paving Corporation had landed a sizable project. Its only solution was to buy a small (50 ton per day output) asphalt plant. This not only helped it competitively in bidding more paving jobs, but in addition the plant could be used in turning out mastic for flooring jobs.

In 1949, Daniel Swartz authorized the purchase of their first real asphalt plant, specifically a Hetherington & Berner 2000-pound batch plant. With this move, Lake Erie Asphalt Paving Corporation was in a new competitive field. The prices for paving per square foot went down instead of up. Efficiency, therefore, became a still more important factor. Furthermore, big jobs were needed to utilize this new one-ton plant to the fullest extent. In order to do work for the State Highway Department, a company must be prequalified; it took three years to acquire this prequalification, and the company continued to do small jobs in this interim. After prequalification in 1952, most of the emphasis was placed on paving; waterproofing and floor mastic jobs were forgotten.

In 1954, a new two-ton Hetherington & Berner batch plant was purchased, and a portable Barber-Greene continuous-mix plant was acquired in 1956. At this time, the competition in bidding was very keen; union wages were another important factor in bidding.

In 1959, the Lake Erie Asphalt Paving Corporation still had three asphalt plants located in Detroit, South Lyon, and Iosco County. The organization chart of the company appears in Exhibit I.

Exhibit I

ORGANIZATIONAL CHART

LAKE ERIE ASPHALT PAVING CO.

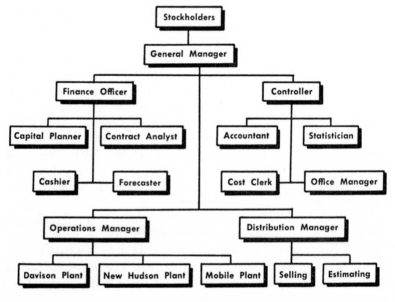

THE COMPANY

The corporation is both a manufacturing and a construction-contracting firm, with its basic interest in the asphalt for public projects. By "public" is meant any federal, state, county, municipality, or township road paving project. A percentage of the business comes from past reputation in paving parking lots and drives in residential, industrial, and commercial areas.

The new Federal Housing Administration law requiring all subdivisions to have paved streets and roads before FHA approval of any housing mortgage has widened the corporation's scope of operations. Earth moving, excavation, grading, and base installation are now part of the asphalt paving business. These add a greater need for a closely controlled corporate system.

CAPACITY

The present capacity for the manufacturing of asphaltic materials is governed by the size of the three asphalt plants. The Detroit plant is rated at two (2) tons per minute, or approximately 960 tons of material per day. The South Lyons plant is rated at one (1) ton per minute, or 480 tons per day. In addition to these two plants, the portable one is a one (1) ton plant. This gives an over-all material production capacity of 240,000 tons a season. The season is calculated by taking an average of 20 working days a month for six months, or 120 working days. The season is limited by state regulations, which prohibits truck traffic before all the frost has disappeared from the ground; past experience dates this around May 15. The end of the season is determined by the state's specifications, which limit the installation of asphaltic materials to days when temperatures are 50 degrees or higher; this date is around November 1 to November 15.

SALES POTENTIAL

The capacities and the corporation's other assets are used by the state in qualifying each contractor. A rating by the state is necessary before making bids on state projects. The reasoning behind this is as follows: The state prefers to distribute its work among all the qualified paving contractors, and this system is about the fairest. The state first determines what amount of money will be spent on road construction during the coming year. After this is published, it proportions a company's assets to the combined assets of all the other contractors. This proportioned figure then represents the amount of work a particular company will be qualified to do for the state in the coming season. As stated, this is a potential and not a guarantee. The only stipulation the county applies to bidders is that they be state prequalified. The city of Detroit, however, allows everybody and anybody to bid on its projects.

Another sales potential, as mentioned above, stems from the FHA's requirement that all roads be paved if a FHA mortgage is to be granted. This requires a greater outlay of capital by the subdivision owner before any type of return can be realized. Asphaltic roads are cheaper and more durable than cement-concrete roads, giving the company the edge in this area.[1] Thus, asphalt paving is tied to the building trend, federal spending for new roads, and other public spending on maintenance and revisions.

Since no historical data can ever predict how many jobs will be forthcoming, the company must figure on a single-job basis. Perhaps the past experience of Daniel Swartz will be able to determine exactly what kind of economic conditions are in store when forecasts for 1959 predict: "Highway construction: federal-state program ($102 billion, 41,000 miles) has been getting under way very slowly but will speed up during 1959. It will be significant for many businesses, in many locations."

Since potentials are set up in an area only by being competitive, and the secret to competition is to reduce labor and material costs, the ideal situation is to have the asphalt manufacturing plant located in a sand and gravel pit, while having the contracted job within a five-mile radius. Under this ideal situation, most of the handling and trucking necessary in the manufacturing of asphaltic materials can be eliminated.

MANUFACTURED PRODUCT

There are two major classifications for the manufactured product of an asphalt plant. These products are classified as asphaltic concrete and bituminous aggregate. The asphaltic concretes are

---

[1] Asphaltic-concrete road building is still in its infancy.

used to resurface rigid pavements, whereas bituminous aggregate is used over a flexible base. The asphaltic concretes call for a stone which has been washed and is 50 per cent crushed. The bituminous aggregate uses gravel instead of stone, and it does not have to be crushed. Crushing supposedly retains the asphaltic cements better; that is, there are more "faces" to hold.

The materials used to make asphaltic concrete are: coarse and fine stone, coarse and fine sand, fly ash, and asphaltic cement. The percentages are: 60 per cent stone, 30 per cent sand, 5 per cent fly ash (mineral filler), and 5 per cent asphalt. Primarily, the mix is comprised of approximately 93 per cent miscellaneous materials and 7 per cent asphaltic cements.

THE MANFACTURING PLANT

Materials are manufactured through the following process (Exhibit II). The aggregate and sand are dumped into a hopper, where they are transferred to the drier by means of the "cold" elevator. After the materials traverse the entire length of the drier, they are transported to the top of the plant by means of the "hot" elevator. The materials are run through the drier in order to remove some moisture and to heat the stone so that the asphaltic cement will be retained better. These materials are now screened into three different bins, and the mineral filler added. From these bins, the operator or the automatic controls dumps the correct amount (by weight) of material from the weight bucket into the pugmill. At this stage the asphaltic cement is added and mixed for approximately 45 to 60 seconds. After mixing, this whole batch is dropped immediately into a truck. This process is repeated until the truck is filled; single-axle trucks can only carry 5 to 7 tons without being charged a penalty by the union rates. A tandem-axle truck can carry 12 tons.

Hereafter the company is converted from a manufacturing company into a construction firm. The asphaltic concrete now has to be laid on the street, road, or roadway to be resurfaced. The truck backs up into a mechanical spreader (Exhibit III). The spreader is self-propelled and travels at different rates of speeds, as directed by the inspector, with a maximum of 60 feet per minute. The width of the mat is usually 10 feet but can be adjusted to lay 5 to 12 feet. The thickness of the mat is

Exhibit II

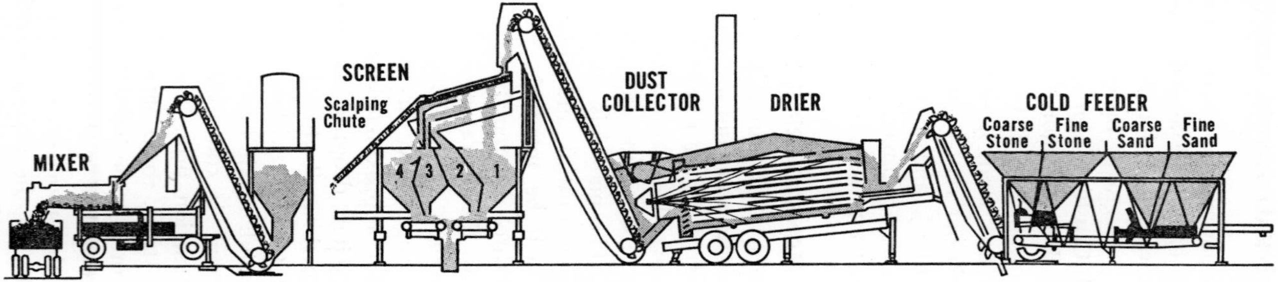

ASPHALT PLANT

MIXER

SCREEN
Scalping Chute

DUST COLLECTOR

DRIER

COLD FEEDER
Coarse Stone | Fine Stone | Coarse Sand | Fine Sand

Exhibit III

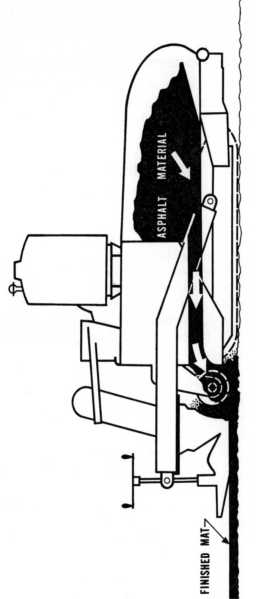

ASPHALT MATERIAL

FINISHED MAT

MECHANICAL SPREADER

directly adjusted by a screw on the back of the spreader; the range is from ½ inch to approximately 4 inches. The placed material is then rolled by means of a powered roller of different weights, depending on the design of the job.

DELIVERY REQUIREMENTS AND INVENTORIES

The materials needed for the manufacturing of asphaltic concrete can be delivered as the jobs are acquired, eliminating the necessity for any inventories either at the beginning or at the end of the season.

OVERHEAD

Daniel Swartz feels that "The final results of the sales forecast can be summed up as follows: Overhead expenses can be met only out of contract earnings (assuming there is no other source of income). Job estimates for bids should allow for this factor. Therefore, the business should be conducted to show a profit after deducting overhead expenses from gross profits realized on contracts. This would then lead to the conclusion that the overhead expenses should be controlled to fit the available volume of business and there may be periods when there will not be a sufficient volume available to support a minimum overhead, that is, one based on maintaining a skeleton force. There is no accurate gauge to measure proper overhead charges in either dollars or percentages to business volume. The president and the general manager receive this responsibility to determine prudently a successful operational charge for each contract."

EARTH MOVING

Earth moving is just one phase of the business, and it might give a little better picture of how difficult estimating a job in construction can be. Efficiency tends to be whittled down by a combination of factors, each seemingly minor, and a small percentage of improvements "all along the line" will add up to a substantial production increase and a reduction in costs.

The measure of a machine, a plant, a man, or a dirt-moving job is *efficiency*. Some of these factors are easy to appraise, others difficult. The elements that go into the total make-up of a construction project are not only often difficult to predict, but when added together can combine to a rather staggering total.

As a 100 per cent starting point, the contractor has a given number of working days in any calendar period. The first obstacle to efficiency he faces is one of delays to either all or part of the operation; these delays are due to items which the contractor can anticipate but which involve difficulty in controlling. These include weather preceding construction, engineering not finished on schedule, absenteeism on the part of the crews, etc. The efficiency of any of these factors may vary from almost nothing for short periods up to 50 per cent or more in an extremely wet season. To see how a total project can suffer, let us assign 10 per cent to these causes as a starter and look further.

In the 90 per cent time remaining, the equipment spread — whether scrapers and push tractors, truck and shovels, or paving layout — is subject to mechanical breakdowns. Some of these may overlap in the repair time with weather or other down time, but an extra loss of 5 per cent to 15 per cent, depending upon conditions of equipment, maintenance program, and job conditions, may well be anticipated. If this is only 5 per cent, the efficiency is now down to 85.5 per cent (90 $\times$ 95).

Next, a big bite comes in what is known as the 50-minute hour. This factor is simply the recognition that over a period of time an equipment operator and the conditions of a job seldom combine to produce more than 50 actual working minutes out of 60. Although 55-minute efficiency is sometimes recorded, a range between 40 and 50 minutes out of 60 is usually encountered. Complete balance of hauling to loading units is difficult, if not impossible; as a result, there is some waiting at cut or fill, units sometimes bog down, operators stop for a drink, instruction, or a breather.

The result of this factor can be measured by checking a load count for a given period and comparing it against the average of cycle times for the same period on all the uninterrupted cycles. For example, if units can average 4-minute cycles, the indicated load count would be 15 per hour per machine. A 2-hour load count simultaneous with timed cycles showing 25 loads actually hauled would be at a 50-minute hour, or $^{25}\!/_{30} = 83$ per cent efficiency. Total efficiency at this point is down to 70.9 per cent (85.5×83).

Still another, but not so easily defined element in efficiency, takes an additional toll. This factor is the difference between the average hauling cycle and some shorter cycle or faster production rate which might be achieved. The graph (Exhibit IV) il-

Exhibit IV

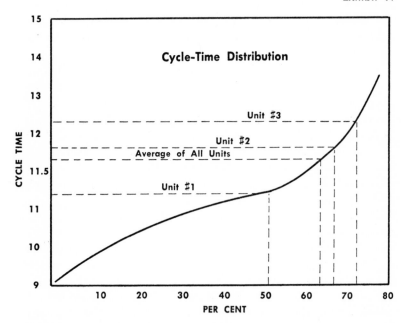

Cycle-Time Distribution

CYCLE TIME

PER CENT

lustrates how cycle times may vary on a given haul with three scrapers working. In this case the longest cycle time was 16 minutes and the shortest about 9.5 minutes. The average load, haul, spread, and return cycle for each machine is marked separately and the combined average also shown.

To use the graph, read the over-all average point to the left-hand scale, which shows a cycle time of 11.6 minutes. Reading down from the same point on the curve to the per-cent scale at the bottom shows that of all the loads hauled, 63 per cent

Exhibit V

THE LAKE ERIE ASPHALT PAVING CORPORATION
PROFIT AND LOSS STATEMENT
FOR THE YEARS ENDED DECEMBER 31, 1958 AND 1957

	YEAR ENDED DECEMBER 31			
	1958		1957	
SALES:	$	$1,932,403.45	$	$1,651,433.33
Cost of Sales:				
Inventory	11,851.20		7,350.45	
Materials	792,433.60		641,426.64	
Labor	386,428.36		336,587.50	
Hired Trucking	102,969.38		112,498.38	
Equipment Rental	139,959.92		86,801.11	
Equipment Operation	73,649.12		75,415.33	
Equip. Repairs	38,127.30		38,156.47	
Heat, Light, and Power	10,163.34		9,210.53	
Depreciation — Equipment	63,801.35		64,110.26	
Depreciation — Building	2,130.35		2,098.12	
Total	$1,621,513.92		$1,373,654.69	
Less Inventory, Dec. 31	7,994.80	1,613,519.12	11,851.20	1,361,803.49
Cost of Sales		$ 338,884.33		$ 289,629.84
Operating Expenses:				
Executive and Administrative Salaries	$ 139,290.65		$ 135,371.98	
Advertising	4,819.01		4,539.58	
Insurance	14,236.26		8,030.65	
Telephone — Telegraph	5,108.43		4,878.07	
Traveling	18,981.73		13,797.30	
Association Dues, Subscription and Donation	8,784.41		7,574.00	
Contributions to Union Welfare, Pensions, and Insurance Funds	11,148.00		3,050.00	
Office, Professional Fees and Sundry	6,919.19		7,229.46	
Bad Debts	14,478.79		7,183.00	
Taxes Other Than Income: Social Security and Unemployment	24,330.79		20,912.28	
Property and Other Corporate Taxes	25,182.80	273,280.06	24,748.31	237,314.63
Total Operating Expenses		$ 65,604.27		$ 52,315.21
Other Income:				
Scrap Sales	$ 2,051.15		$ 533.21	
Purchase Discounts	7,041.45		4,983.34	
Interest	143.50	9,236.10	79.97	5,596.52
		$ 74,840.37		$ 57,911.73
Other Expenses:				
Interest	$ 3,974.97		$ 2,717.33	
Discounts	504.37	4,479.34	1,925.29	4,642.62
NET PROFIT BEFORE TAXES		$ 70,361.03		$ 53,269.11

were on shorter cycles times than the average. The graph also shows for comparison that unit No. 3 averaged 12.15 minute cycles, and about 73 per cent of all loads hauled were faster than this individual machine's average. The efficiency problem here is more difficult. But it is possible to read up from the

Exhibit VI

THE LAKE ERIE ASPHALT PAVING CORPORATION — BALANCE SHEETS
DECEMBER 31, 1958, 1957

ASSETS

	1958 Cost	1958 Depreciation	1958 Net	1957 Cost	1957 Depreciation	1957 Net
Current Assets						
Cash in Bank and on Hand			$ 79,361.78			$ 74,401.39
Notes Receivable			1,500.00			2,300.00
Accounts Receivable:						
Construction			$413,145.70			$367,374.69
Deposits on Bids			1,800.00			5,250.00
Prepayments, Claims, Employees Sundry			3,522.50			25,996.30
			$418,468.20			$398,620.99
Less Reserve for Bad Debts			2,118.21			2,118.21
			416,349.99			396,502.78
Inventory			7,994.80			11,851.20
Total Current Assets			$505,206.57			$485,055.37
Plant & Equipment						
Land	$ 48,748.41	$ -0-	$ 48,748.41	$ 48,748.41	$ -0-	$ 48,748.41
Building	47,964.02	14,962.13	33,001.89	47,810.30	12,831.78	34,978.52
Machinery and Equipment	414,095.45	275,094.19	139,001.26	377,110.65	234,963.33	142,147.32
	$510,807.88	$290,056.32	$220,751.56	$473,669.36	$247,795.11	$225,874.25
Total Plant and Equipment			220,751.56			225,874.25
Total Assets			$725,958.13			$710,929.62

LIABILITIES AND CAPITAL

	1958		1957	
Current Liabilities				
Notes Payable:				
Bank	$ 40,000.00		$ 40,000.00	
Bank — Equipment Notes	13,903.92		1,400.00	
		$ 53,909.92		$ 41,400.00
Accounts Payable		168,720.45		162,053.53
Accrued Compensation		3,960.00		42,102.92
Accrued Taxes		21,144.45		20,982.78
Accrued Income Tax		31,087.74		24,686.91
Total Current Liabilities		$278,822.56		$291,226.14
Capital				
Capital Stock		$ 6,750.00		$ 6,740.00
Earned Surplus January 1	$401,112.28		$384,381.28	
Net Profit for 1 Year	39,273.29		28,582.20	
		440,385.57		412,963.48
Total Capital Stock and Surplus		447,135.57		419,703.48
Total Liabilities and Capital		$725,958.13		$710,929.62

bottom scale at 50 per cent and across to 11.2 minutes and say — assuming one machine can average this time, and half of all loads hauled are faster — that all units might well have the same average. At the extreme, it is difficult to believe that one load hauled in 9.5 minutes constitutes any demonstrated ability to average 9.5 minutes. Somewhere in between, however, is an attainable higher average. If in this instance it was determined that, since 30 per cent of the cycle were faster than 10.85 minutes, this represented an obtainable figure, then the indicated working efficiency at the average shown is about 93 per cent.

The curve actually represents a smooth-running operation with 40 per cent of the loads hauled falling into a time spread of 10.5 to 11.5 minutes, and would be a tough one to change substantially. Nevertheless, if the faster cycle is practical, then the indicated efficiency is at 93 per cent for this phase, and the total finally becomes 70.9 × 93 or about 66 per cent. The significant point is that over-all job efficiency is the result of a number of factors. Each is taking a slice from a rapidly declining potential to produce. The organization that combines its operating know-how to save a per cent or two, all the way down the line, can well achieve the difference between a "going concern" (Exhibits V and VI) and one having trouble with the job.

VI. THE EXCELSIOR TIRE COMPANY

THE Excelsior Tire Company was founded in Lansing, Michigan, by Messrs. John Samuelson and Robert Connell in April, 1956. It was originally known as Excelsior Tire Sales and Service. Mr. Samuelson and Mr. Connell leased a Pure Service Station on one of the main streets of the city. Their capital investment was $2,000. The objective of the founders of the company was not merely to engage in the wholesale sale of tires, batteries, and other accessories, but to expand into such fields as television, radio, refrigerator, lawn equipment, and the like. They realized this goal to some extent within a span of about two years.

Mr. Samuelson was a young man with determination and willingness to work. He became the president. Mr. Connell, also in his early twenties, became the vice-president. Mr. Samuelson had graduated from the School of Business of the University of Chicago and had three years' experience working with the Goodrich Tire Company as a salesman. Mr. Connell's experience was more in the service-repairs field. A cousin of Mr. Samuelson, Elda Rodin, was appointed as treasurer and a sister of Mr. Connell, Miss Marie Connell, was appointed secretary.

There were the usual initial difficulties in the running of the business, but there were hopes for a better future. In December of 1956, a major decision was made to move the operations of the company to a better locale. The company shifted to a store 20 by 120 feet on a side street off the same main street, with greater facilities for parking and service.

An additional $2,000 was raised as working capital. With the notable increase in sales and consequent need for greater purchases, an even greater need was felt for working capital. Mr. Connell found it impossible to help any further in this matter. A meeting was then called of the Samuelson brothers: Kenneth, Robert, Charles, James, and John. It was decided to purchase Robert Connell's stock from Excelsior Tire Sales and Service. This was accomplished and the company was given a new name: The Excelsior Tire Company. Mr. John Samuelson was retained

Exhibit I

THE EXCELSIOR TIRE COMPANY
BALANCE SHEET
DECEMBER 31, 1958, AND MARCH 31, 1959

ASSETS	December 31, 1958		March 31, 1959	
Current Assets:				
Cash on Hand and in Bank	$ 572.57		$ 5,913.27	
Accounts Receivable	17,833.47		20,011.56	
Subscriptions Receivable	8,100.00		8,100.00	
Inventory	59,856.90		58,402.03	
Prepaid Insurance	198.93		589.31	
Total Current Assets		$86,561.87		$93,016.17
Deposits		895.00		895.00
Fixed Assets:				
Office Furniture and Fixtures (Less Reserve)	$ 1,048.73		$ 1,017.53	
Machinery and Equipment (Net)	803.82		1,027.75	
Delivery Equipment (Net)	1,416.47		1,227.95	
Total Fixed Assets		3,269.02		3,273.23
Total Assets		$90,725.89		$97,184.40
LIABILITIES AND CAPITAL				
Current Liabilities:				
Accounts Payable	$65,816.02		$72,310.44	
Loan Payable	6,400.00		5,200.00	
Withholding and Social Security Taxes Payable	578.15		417.68	
Michigan Unemployment Taxes Payable	41.38		227.36	
Federal Unemployment Taxes Payable	44.90		25.26	
Accrued Michigan Sales Tax	623.97		395.82	
Accrued Michigan Business Activities Tax	115.63			
Accrued Property Taxes			120.00	
Provision for Federal Income Tax			406.00	
Total Current Liabilities		$73,620.05		$79,132.56
Stockholders' Equity (Capital):				
Capital Stock — Common, 5000 shares Authorized, $10.00 Par Value Issued and Outstanding — 1800 Shares		18,000.00		18,000.00
Surplus		(894.16)		51.84
Total Liabilities and Capital		$90,725.89		$97,184.40

as president and was also made treasurer. Mr. Kenneth Samuelson, John's older brother, was made vice-president and secretary. The reorganized corporation was set up in March, 1957, with a sum of $10,000 as working capital.

Business boomed from $8,000 sales a month to $13,000 with the full-time employment of John and Kenneth Samuelson, and two service attendants. The service help mainly consisted of delivery, putting on or taking off tires from cars, care of used tires, automobile repairs of a minor nature, and so on. By now, the newly formed management had decided to take on a limited amount of retailing business as well.

Quarterly meetings of the board of directors consisting of all the Samuelson brothers were held to decide on broad policies

Exhibit II

THE EXCELSIOR TIRE COMPANY
INCOME STATEMENT
PERIODS ENDED DECEMBER 31, 1958, AND MARCH 31, 1959

	December 31, 1958		March 31, 1959	
Sales	$256,174.99		$ 83,108.81	
Less Sales Tax	2,673.68		1,175.28	
Net Sales		$253,501.31		$81,933.53
Cost of Goods Sold:				
Inventory, 1/1/58–1/1/59	$ 12,575.96		$ 59,856.90	
Purchases	253,116.37		65,583.35	
Total	$265,692.33		$125,440.25	
Freight In	41.58			
Total	$265,733.91		$125,440.25	
Inventory, 12/31/58–3/31/59	59,856.90		58,402.03	
Cost of Goods Sold		$205,877.01		$67,038.22
Gross Margin		$ 47,624.30		$14,895.31
Selling, General and Administrative Expenses:				
Officers' Salaries	$ 14,225.00		$ 3,900.00	
Salaries — Service and Sales	12,209.00		3,955.90	
Office Salaries	872.06		565.00	
Contract Labor and Service	3,604.19		609.52	
Rent	4,100.00		1,050.00	
Auto and Truck Expense	1,279.74		357.57	
Advertising	3,832.70		805.45	
Travel and Entertainment	297.27		19.75	
Salesmen's Expenses	695.00		. . . . . .	
Payroll Taxes	1,145.26		474.93	
Taxes — General	356.25		388.59	
Licenses and Permits	119.85		17.50	
Insurance	597.85		170.30	
Office Supplies and Expense	411.21		64.32	
Telephone and Telegraph	958.97		217.75	
Heat and Light	863.19		133.98	
Legal and Accounting	470.03		382.38	
Interest Expense	314.85		218.86	
Depreciation	1,147.56		286.89	
Dues and Subscriptions	68.00			
Contributions	35.00			
Miscellaneous Expenses	138.84		249.59	
Shop Supplies and Expenses	339.96			
Uniforms and Laundry	321.70			
Total Expenses		48,403.48		$13,868.28
Net Profit (Loss) From Operations		(779.18)		1,027.03
Miscellaneous Income				324.97
Net Income Before Taxes				$ 1,352.00
Provision for Federal Income Taxes				406.00
Net Income (Loss)		$ (779.18)		$ 946.00

and expand the operations of the company. Thus, the suggestion by the president, John Samuelson, to carry Motorola products was approved, together with the usual tires and accessories. It was also decided in one of the board meetings to get into a mutually profitable agreement with an outstanding tire-manufacturing company. After the necessary inquiries, it was found that the Goodrich Tire Company offered, in the present circumstances, the best possibilities. Thus, the Excelsior Tire Company began to carry Goodrich rubber products exclusively.

In 1958, the B. F. Goodrich Company offered a loan of $10,000 to the company for two years. This gesture eased the financial situation of the company greatly.

Business grew from $168,000 to $268,000 from 1958 to 1959. With the growth of business, there was a corresponding growth in clerical and bookkeeping work. Consequently, an office girl was employed on a full-time basis in order that the president and the vice-president could concentrate their attention more fully on the general welfare of the business. It became evident that with the expansion of business into other fields and a greater inventory, there was a clear need for more floor space. For a second time, a major decision with regard to location became a necessity. In March, 1958, this change was effected; the company shifted its quarters to a 150 by 50-foot store almost opposite the present store. The new quarters also had a full basement, and parking facilities for nearly 200 cars.

A clearer understanding of the financial aspects of the operations of the company may be gleaned by examining and interpreting Exhibits I and II.

VII. WALTERS JEWELRY

WALTERS JEWELRY is a retail credit jewelry and optical firm. It was founded in 1933 by Dr. Harold Walters, an optometrist, and was called Ideas Jewelry. Ideas Jewelry was a small store and operations were devoted primarily to the practice of Dr. Walters' profession as an optometrist.

In December of 1935, Dr. Walters moved his operations to quarters in the main business district of Highland Park, Michigan, the present location of the store. At the same time, the store's name was changed to Walters Jewelry. Success in the new location was moderate until 1939, when a period of growth began which has continued to the present.

CUSTOMER POLICY

Walters has always followed the policy of building a clientele of regular and satisfied customers who would not only patronize the store for all their jewelry needs, but also send their friends to the store. This policy has been effected through various means. Dr. Walters encourages employees to remember customers' names and to make every effort to be on a friendly basis with them. High-pressure selling is forbidden and an employee can be fired for attempting it. To avoid this method of selling, no commissions on sales are given. Customers are encouraged to come in and browse around by the use of signs carrying this idea and the salesmen inviting them to come in and look around any time. Refunds are given on any purchase that has not been altered. Salesmen are instructed, however, to make an effort to have the customer accept an exchange or a due bill. The store does not have a delivery service. Purchases are wrapped for mailing at no charge and employees have taken it upon themselves, on an individual basis, to make deliveries if it will aid in satisfying the customer. Many items of service such as minor repairs to jewelry, replacing lost screws in glasses, and minor watch adjustments are given at no charge. This practice has often been responsible for making loyal customers out of people who had no previous contact with the store. Boxes and gift wrapping are also given with all purchases at no charge.

PERSONNEL

Dr. Walters has always operated his store with a very low rate of labor turnover. Mr. Haumschild, the manager, has been with the firm for eight years; Mrs. Rice, bookkeeper, five and one-half years; Mrs. Gary, credit collection, six years; Mrs. Ringé, saleswoman, fourteen years; Mr. Hapalla, salesman, seven years; and Willie, porter, sixteen years. The maintaining of long-term employment can be credited to the respect held for Dr. Walters by his employees and the "one-happy-family idea" he promotes. Seldom does Dr. Walters give an order. If he wants something done he asks the employee if he would mind doing him a favor or he puts it in the form of a suggestion. During Christmas week he arranges for food catering service in the store, and this creates a party atmosphere and demonstrates his appreciation for the long hours and extra work put in during the holiday season. A two-week vacation with pay, a week's pay as a Christmas bonus, and the paying of one half of the Blue Cross insurance by the firm are among employee benefits. Employees work under conditions where they know what their duties are and they are left pretty much on their own. There is no one standing over them to see what they are doing. When a conflict develops between employees, Dr. Walters generally allows them to settle their differences without interference on his part.

CLIENTELE

The store's clientele, for the most part, is composed of people in the lower-income groups. Many are from the South who have migrated to Detroit and the suburban areas to work in the automobile industry. The store also enjoys considerable trade from employees of local firms.

Although the store has operated successfully by cultivating this trade, it has not been without problems. Sales are affected considerably by a decline whenever there is a strike or layoff in the automobile industry. The class of trade limits sales, in most instances, to medium-price and low-price goods which often do not carry as large a profit margain as high-price goods. The dollar margin obtained per sale is also smaller; this is offset in part, however, by volume. Moreover, the nature of the goods as mostly luxury items makes the store extremely sensitive to declines in the economy and employment. During periods of such decline many of the store's customers return to their native states, discontinue their purchases, and increase the risk of extending credit.

CREDIT

Credit is extended quite liberally with 48 to 50 per cent of sales being made on a credit basis. The criterion used in granting credit is a steady income and the intent to pay. All applications for credit are cleared through Michigan Merchants, a retail credit clearinghouse, of which the firm is a member. Such clearance allows the firm to obtain additional information on the applicants' intent to pay. It provides information on previous applications for credit, promptness in payment, and cases of nonpayment. This information is then checked against their applications in determining the acceptability of the risk.

Terms offered on credit sales are a minimum of 10 per cent down and a 10 per cent carrying charge on the balance, which is deducted if the account is paid in ninety days. On diamond and watch sales, the carrying charge is deducted if the account is paid within the time the credit has been extended.

Bad debts fluctuate between 5 to 7 per cent of credit sales. This is due to the reluctance of Dr. Walters to dun the customers within a short period after they miss a payment, which gives the customer time to move before he is dunned. Then, when aggressive action is taken to collect the account it becomes more difficult and more expensive to collect.

In January, 1956, action was taken to correct the bad-debt loss. The taking and clearing of applications became more thorough, statements were mailed within two weeks of a missed payment, and customers who did not respond within a period of six statements were turned over to the U. S. Credit Bureau, a collection agency. If a customer is laid off, sick, or has some other legitimate reason for not making his payments, no action is taken to collect the account as long as he keeps in touch with the store.

ADVERTISING

Since 1952, Walters has advertised extensively. Current advertising costs from 6 to 8 per cent of gross sales. The advertising media is primarily spot radio, weekly newspapers, and direct mail.

Until the beginning of 1957, radio advertising had consisted of two daily spot announcements on the afternoon hillbilly program, Sagebrush Melodies. In 1957, radio advertising was increased to four spot announcements of 100 words each. This program was used to introduce the Doc's Famous Fifty and Honeymoon Hundred diamond sets which were well accepted by the listeners. The program was also used to introduce Walters' watches, the company's private brand.[1]

Newspaper advertising is done in three weekly papers: *The Highland Parker, North End News,* and the *Ferndale News.* A weekly insertion of an optical advertisement is made and the jewelry ad varies from week to week with the items advertised. In the past, full-page ads carrying a variety of items have been used for the three weeks preceding Christmas.

Direct mail has been used to blanket areas selected by zones on the basis of trade received from each zone and has also been used exclusively for the firm's own mailing list. The direct-mail advertising consists of pieces supplied by manufacturers and by the firm.

The firm's means of checking the effectiveness of advertising is to rely on the number of customers mentioning it and to ask customers why they come in for a particular item if it is being advertised at the time.

COMPETITION

Walters Jewelry operates under highly competitive conditions. In Highland Park there are six other jewelry stores. Of the six, three are chain operations. The company is also in competition with two department stores: Sears Roebuck and Penneys. Sears has a complete jewelry department, whereas Penneys carries only watches, costume jewelry, and men's jewelry. In addition, a majority of the men's and women's shops carry either costume jewelry

---

[1] Walters' watches presently accounts for about 19 per cent of total watch sales.

or men's jewelry. Since 1953, Walters has been faced with very serious competition from the so-called "public wholesale outlets" or "discount houses." Two discount houses are located across the street from Walters.

Competition from legitimate retailers was met through maintaining a good reputation for ethics, fair prices, providing service for all goods sold, and treating all customers fairly. Aggressive advertising and promotion and liberal credit terms were also used in meeting this competition. Competition in the handling of costume and men's jewelry was met by handling exclusive lines in Highland Park such as Anson, DeVers Creations, House of Rosseau, and the like. Items such as cultured pearls, gold-filled and sterling jewelry were added since they were typically handled by jewelers, carried the firm's name on the box, and offered higher margins.

Competition from the discount houses was considered impossible to meet on a price basis. Discount houses offered prices on nationally advertised goods which were in many instances below dealer cost or only slightly above (see Exhibit I).

Since the store is located in a high-rent district, customers expected many services which would send them to other merchants if discontinued. Insufficient space in the present location for volume precluded the possibility of operating as a discount house. In addition, such an operation did not appeal to Dr. Walters for many other reasons. First, the store was still profitable although the net profit had been reduced. Second, the increasing establishment of discount houses was limiting the market. Some of the people who had purchased items that were not nationally advertised in these outlets indicated that what was lost on nationally advertised goods had to be made up on goods the customers could not compare. Third, this type of pricing was against the policy Dr. Walters had always followed of selling an item at a price which would give the customer good value and at the same time provide the business with a reasonable profit.

Walters Jewelry has tried to meet this competition in various ways. On nationally advertised watches it has given extra liberal trade-in allowances which in some cases amount to one third of the price. Discounts have been given to customers who ask for them. Sales on a store-wide basis were held more frequently,

Exhibit I

Comparison of Dealer Costs With Advertised Retail Prices

	Walters' Costs	Discount House Prices*
Schick Electric Razor	$14.62	$ 9.95
Norelco Electric Razor	$12.76	$12.99
Schick 1958 Model	$16.36	$15.47
Remington Rollectric	$16.80	$15.99
Home-Auto Remington	$20.60	$17.99

*Prices as stated in newspaper advertising.

although in all cases prices were not lowered to meet the discount houses. Special order work such as remounting, engraving, and making up of personal jewelry was talked up among customers since the regular margin could still be obtained. Dr. Walters was also on the lookout for new items not available in discount houses which he could add to his lines. In 1953, the Walters brand of watches was introduced.[2] Since 1953, a china department had been added, and imported items which generally carry larger margins than similar American products were sampled in 1957.

The methods used in meeting competition are felt to have been responsible for the firm's being able to maintain itself, and from 1954 through 1956 to increase its volume slightly. The margin of profit during this period, however, has declined over 1½ per cent.

---

[2] Walters' watches have the same movement as many of the nationally advertised brands and carry a lifetime guarantee as long as they are cleaned once a year.

VIII. THE CITY OF INDUSTRY

TREND OF GENERAL CITY EXPENDITURES

GREAT demands for more services and spending have been placed on the government of the City of Industry. The pressures of these demands are a result of both internal and external forces. Internally they come from the citizens of the municipality. In addition, the rapidly growing surrounding area has placed demands on the resources of the City of Industry. Exhibit I shows a marked upward trend in total appropriations from 1947 through 1958. Total appropriations have increased from 112.3 million dollars in 1947 to 235.2 million dollars in 1958. This is an increase of 109.4 per cent above fiscal 1947.

Pension costs have soared. The appropriation of 22.7 million dollars in fiscal year 1958 represents a 278.3 per cent increase over the appropriation of 6 million dollars in fiscal 1947. Other appropriations for 1958 have increased as follows: salaries and wages, 107.6 per cent; material and supplies, 88.4 per cent; improvements, 129.4 per cent; and debt service, 38.4 per cent.

Percentage increase in salaries and wages is only slightly less than the percentage increase in total appropriations. However, when the two personnel costs, pensions and salaries and wages are combined, the increase in the total of these two appropriations for 1958 is 124.5 per cent above the 1947 level. Therefore, personnel costs absorb 58 per cent of total appropriations in 1958 as compared to 54 per cent in 1947.

The foregoing review of expenditures shows there is a marked upward trend of costs and there is no indication that this trend is abating. In fact, there is a growing tendency for government to become more expensive. In addition to the general inflationary trend, other factors contributing to this rise are: costs that outrun the increases in population, cost of living, increase in the number of city employees per 1000 population, and the City of Industry's metropolitan responsibilities.

Although it may be argued that these expenditures are necessary to produce higher standards of government, at the same time it should be recognized that the financial resources of the City of Industry are not unlimited.

CAPITAL EXPENDITURES

Exhibit II shows that capital facility needs extend to almost all divisions of the city's operations. However, Exhibit III shows that there has been a change in the method used to finance this capital program. In fiscal year (Fy.) 1955–1956 more bonds were used to finance the City of Industry's capital improvement program than at any other time in the postwar period. A declining amount of current revenue is being used. The percentage of capital expenditure financed by bonds has increased from 0 per cent in fiscal year 1947–1948 to 63.48 per cent in 1955–1956.

Financing policy for the City of Industry's capital improvements has never been explicitly formulated. From the completely pay-as-you-go policy followed in 1947–1948, there has been a shift to a modified pay-as-you-go policy. In the mayor's budget message to the common council on April 2, 1954, this policy was defined as follows:

> These bond authorizations are in keeping with our modified pay-as-you-go policy of paying for over half of the capital improvements out of current revenues, and paying for part of the capital improvements out of bond proceeds, but at the same time retiring more bonds than we are issuing.[1]

The following years the budget message referred to:

> . . . our policy of paying for appropriate capital improvements with bonds, but at the same time retiring more bonds than are issued.[2]

It should be noted that reference to "paying for over half of the capital improvements out of the current revenues" has been omitted as a part of the modified pay-as-you-go policy. In addition, the term "appropriate capital improvements" is not clearly defined. A wide variety of such expenditures could be justified under this policy.

Again, on April 10, 1956, the budget message stated:

> It is still planned to stay within our past policy of not issuing more faith and credit bonds than we are retiring.[3]

---

[1] *Journal of the Common Council*, April 2, 1954, p. 778.

[2] *Ibid.*, April 12, 1955, p. 642.

[3] *Ibid.*, April 10, 1956, p. 643.

It seems that the policy of using current revenue for more than one half of these expenditures has been discarded. Moreover, in both fiscal years 1956 and 1957 City of Industry bonded debt increased, indicating that more faith and credit bonds were issued than were retired.

In summary, it would appear that the City of Industry's policy for financing capital improvements has consisted of the following:

1. Over half of the expenditures should be financed from current revenue.
2. In any one year, more bonds should be retired than are issued thereby reducing the city's bonded debt.
3. Appropriate capital improvements only should be financed through the proceeds of bonds.

SOURCES OF REVENUE

The City of Industry derives its revenue from the following sources:

1. Property taxes — levied upon land, buildings, and personal property within the city.
2. Grants and shared taxes from other governments.
3. Licenses, fines, forfeits, and fees.
4. Miscellaneous taxes and collections.
5. Sales, and reimbursements for services and property.
6. Proceeds from the sale of bonds.
7. General fund contribution to the library — an interfund transfer made annually since 1951.

A comparison of revenue by these major categories for fiscal years 1947 and 1958 is shown in Exhibit IV. During this period, total revenue has more than doubled, increasing from 112.4 million dollars in 1947 to 231.3 million dollars in 1958. The increase in revenue from property taxes was, however, less than the increase in total revenues. Whereas total revenues increased 105.9 per cent, revenue from property taxes increased 78.1 per cent. On the other hand, one new source of revenue, bonds, entered the picture in 1958. These two trends, a decreasing portion of revenue produced by property taxes and an increasing portion produced by bonds, stand out.

Property taxes, nevertheless, have continued to be the major source of income for the city. Revenue from shared taxes and grants come from motor vehicle, gas taxes, and the state sales taxes. The City of Industry's share is dependent largely upon its size relative to the size of the rest of the state, as distribution to villages, cities, and townships is on the basis of population as determined by the decennial federal census. Recalculations, due in 1960, are expected to change the City of Industry's position, as forecasts indicate that the city's share of the total population is decreasing.

Although licenses and fines are a small source of revenue to the city, it is the one item whose yield can be controlled by increasing rates. It offers a possibility for increasing revenue by increasing rates for licenses and permits, and increasing the fines provided for traffic and ordinance violations.

Revenue from sales and reimbursements is largely a result of repayment for hospital and prisoner care, and sales of departmental services. There is some flexibility in the rate structure. However, most of these items are intergovernmental and result merely in interfund transfers to the general fund. In most instances, they do not reflect independent revenues to the city.

CITY RETIREMENT SYSTEMS

The City of Industry maintains two retirement systems for its employees, exclusive of the Board of Education and county employees. The Policemen and Firemen Retirement System was introduced July 1, 1941, and the General City Retirement System, July 1, 1938. When the present systems were initiated several unfunded old plans were in operation. Membership, however, is limited to pensioners on the rolls when the new systems were put into operation, and certain employees who elected to continue membership in the old plans.

Each of the present systems is governed by its own Board of Trustees and benefits for the following are provided: service retirement, duty and nonduty disability, and accidental death benefits for widows and orphans in case of death in the line of duty.

Eligibility for service retirement under the Police and Fire Retirement System is the completion of 25 years of credited service. There is no age stipulation. The benefit consists of a life annuity based on the member's accumulated contributions at retirement plus a pension, paid from city funds, which is the difference between one-half average compensation for the past five years of service, and such life annuity. The city's portion is limited to 15/22 of a patrolman or fire fighter's pay, at present $322.10 per month. Moreover, there is an escalator clause by which the allowance of pensioners is adjusted by any change in the compensation of active members. This is a costly feature and is not normally found in pension planning. Because of the escalator clause, it is impossible to determine and fix the city's liability at the time a member retires.

Reference to Exhibit V shows that none of the nine cities studied have a lower service requirement than the City of In-

Exhibit I

CITY OF INDUSTRY APPROPRIATIONS*
(In Millions)

	1947	1948	1949	1950	1951	1952
Wages and Salaries	$ 54.9	$ 60.8	$ 76.1	$ 70.2	$ 72.0	$ 80.8
Materials, Supplies, and Expense	19.0	22.1	30.3	31.9	31.6	29.9
Operation and Maintenance	73.9	82.9	97.4	102.1	103.6	110.7
Improvements	13.6	13.2	8.7	15.7	19.9	19.2
Debt Service	17.7	17.4	17.5	17.9	18.2	18.4
Pensions	6.0	7.2	7.5	8.2	9.2	10.6
Reserve and Deficit	1.0	1.0	4.9	2.2	1.4	3.3
Total	$112.3	$121.9	$135.9	$146.1	$152.2	$162.2

	1953	1954	1955	1956	1957	1958
Wages and Salaries	$ 88.3	$ 94.4	$ 99.8	$102.8	$108.0	$114.0
Materials, Supplies, and Expense	31.0	29.7	30.4	30.3	34.8	35.8
Operation and Maintenance	119.3	124.1	130.2	133.1	142.8	149.8
Improvements	19.5	22.7	21.9	24.1	37.0	31.2
Debt Service	18.8	19.1	19.5	20.2	21.3	24.5
Pensions	12.6	14.6	16.5	18.7	20.7	22.7
Reserve and Deficit	2.5	1.2	1.2	2.6	1.3	6.9
Total	$172.7	$181.7	$189.2	$198.8	$223.2	$235.2

* Source: *Task Force Report on Trends in Operating Expenditures*, "The City of Industry," p. 6.
Note: The above includes the Library Fund, but excludes the Sewer Bond Fund, debt service on D.S.R., and Water faith and credit bonds, and all revenue supported activities of the city.

Exhibit II

CITY OF INDUSTRY CAPITAL EXPENDITURES BY DEPARTMENTS, 1951–1956, AND APPROPRIATIONS FOR 1957 AND 1958*
(In Thousands of Dollars)

Department	Expenditures Fy. Yrs. 1951–1956	Appropriations Fy. 1957	Fy. 1958
Arts	$ 235	$ 242	$ 30
Aviation	57	24	-0-
Civil Defense	337	-0-	-0-
Election	1,225	475	501
Fire	3,974	400	20
Health	9,434	207	36
Historical	835	7	-0-
House of Correction	-0-	300	-0-
Housing	7,703	750	1,280
Lighting	8,275	3,164	2,326
Memorial Hall	22,220	11,332	9,250
Parks and Recreation	10,189	1,826	782
Police	1,558	509	-0-
Public Works	40,899	10,688	10,074
Recorder's Court	528	186	-0-
Streets and Traffic	3,739	450	21
Welfare	-0-	80	-0-
Zoological Park	317	89	50
Misc. Equipment	3,880	-0-	285
Total General Fund	$115,479	$30,729	$24,655
Library Fund	1,586	2,545	6,500
Sewer Bond Fund	32,073	*	*
Total General City	$149,138	$33,274	$31,155

* SOURCE: *Summary Report, Committee on City Finances,* "City of Industry," p. 15.
NOTES: 1. Housing does not include public housing, only slum clearance and urban renewal.
2. The civic center figures do not include the City of Industry taxpayer's share of the 26,014 thousand dollars for the city-county building, which is owned by a joint city-county authority.
3. Not appropriated; the capital improvement program called for $5,660,000 in fiscal 1957 and $3,485,000 in fiscal 1958.

dustry. Only one city, Boston, pays a higher benefit, and five of the cities studied require higher contributions by the members.

City of Industry employees, in order to be eligible for service retirement, must be sixty years of age, and have a minimum of ten years of credited service. Benefits consist of a life annuity based on the member's contributions, a basic pension of $120 annually, and a pension based on length of service and the member's average compensation of the highest five consecutive years in the past ten. An amendment effective August 13, 1956, extended social-security benefits to City of Industry employees. At age sixty-five, or sixty-two for women, any retirant who has ob-

Exhibit III

SUMMARY TABLE — FINANCING OF THE CITY OF INDUSTRY'S CAPITAL IMPROVEMENT PROGRAM*
Fiscal 1948 to Fiscal 1956 (In Millions)

| Year | Total | Financed by Bonds | | Financed From Current Revenue | |
		Amount	Per Cent	Amount	Per Cent
1947/48	$15.2	$ 0.0	0.00	$15.2	100.0
1948/49	23.9	3.4	14.09	20.5	85.91
1949/50	28.1	9.7	34.60	18.4	65.40
1950/51	21.5	5.7	26.66	15.7	83.34
1951/52	23.9	7.8	32.76	16.1	67.24
1952/53	20.9	7.4	35.31	13.6	64.94
1953/54	23.6	9.7	46.22	13.8	58.80
1954/55	27.7	12.9	46.59	14.8	53.38
1955/56	28.0	17.8	63.48	10.2	36.52

* SOURCE: *Task Force Report on Capital Expenditures and Debt,* "City of Industry," p. 15.

Exhibit IV

REVENUE OF THE CITY OF INDUSTRY FOR THE FISCAL YEARS 1947 AND 1958* (In Millions)

| Revenue Source | Amount of Revenue | | Increase | Per Cent Increase |
	1947	1958		
Property Tax	$ 71.2	$126.8	$ 55.6	78.1
Shared Taxes and Grants	18.6	35.5	16.9	90.9
Licenses, Fines, etc.	4.2	8.5	4.3	102.4
Sales and Reimbursements	17.0	35.8	18.8	110.6
Miscellaneous Taxes	1.4	.5	.9**	-0-
Library (General Fund)	-0-	.6	.6	-0-
Sale of Bonds	-0-	23.4	23.4	-0-
Total	$112.4	$231.3	$118.9	105.9

*SOURCE: *Task Force Report on Revenue Sources,* "City of Industry," pp. 2 and 7.
** Indicates a decrease in revenue.
NOTE: Fiscal year 1947 is actual revenue whereas 1958 is budgeted revenue.

tained his social-security benefits through his city employment will have his city benefit reduced by ten dollars a year for every year of service.

Exhibit VI shows that four cities of the nine studied have a lower eligibility requirement for service retirement. On the other hand, none pay a higher benefit, and five require higher contributions from members.

Exhibit V

COMPARISON OF THE CITY WITH NINE CITIES ON CERTAIN PROVISIONS OF POLICEMEN AND FIREMEN RETIREMENT SYSTEMS*

City	Eligibility for Service Retirement	Rate of Service Retirement Benefit	Rate of Member Contributions
Baltimore	Higher	Lower	About Same
Boston	Higher	Higher	About Same
Chicago	Higher	About Same	Higher
Cleveland	Higher	About Same	Lower
Los Angeles	About Same	About Same	Higher
New York	About Same	About Same	Higher
Philadelphia	Higher	About Same	Higher
St. Louis	Higher	About Same	Lower
San Francisco	Higher	About Same	Higher

* SOURCE: *Summary Report, Committee on City Finances,* "City of Industry," p. 35.

Exhibit VI

COMPARISON OF THE CITY WITH NINE CITIES REGARDING CERTAIN PROVISIONS OF GENERAL EMPLOYEE RETIREMENT SYSTEMS*

City	Eligibility for Service Retirement	Rate of Service Retirement Benefit	Rate of Member Contributions
Baltimore	About Same	Lower	About Same
Boston	Higher	About Same	About Same
Chicago	Lower	Lower	Higher
Cleveland	Lower	Lower	Higher
Los Angeles	About Same	Lower	Higher
New York	Lower	Lower	Higher
Philadelphia	Lower	Lower	About Same
St. Louis	Higher	Lower	Lower
San Francisco	About Same	Lower	Higher

* SOURCE: *Summary Report, Committee on City Finances,* "City of Industry," p. 36.

IX. THE SOUTH SHORE HOSPITAL

THE South Shore Hospital of Chicago, Illinois, was founded in January, 1930, on the southeast side of Chicago by Dr. Michael Walsh, physician and surgeon. Dr. Walsh organized The South Shore Hospital shortly before the untimely death in 1931 of his wife, Mrs. Marion Walsh, R.N.

With some $15,000 of his own capital and a $15,000 loan from the South Shore Bank and Trust Company, Dr. Walsh rented and renovated an old three-story building within walking distance of Lake Michigan, brought equipment and supplies, furnished the rooms according to hospital specifications, and commenced operation with facilities for some forty patients. In addition, Dr. Walsh established an office in the hospital building. Dr. Walsh then appointed Dr. William E. James, a close friend, as assistant director of the hospital. He also hired day and night nurses, a chief cook, a janitor, and other employees.

Scarce information was made available to the case writer as to the administration of the hospital prior to 1955. However, conversations with employees of the hospital who were at the hospital prior to 1955 indicated that virtually all affairs of the hospital, except those under Dr. James, were controlled quite directly during this period by Dr. Walsh. His natural ability to get along with people and his sincere interest in their problems were immeasurable assets in administering the hospital. Yet there were difficulties. Adept in human relations and an excellent physician, Dr. Walsh perhaps did not devote sufficient time to such business affairs of the hospital as inventory control, purchasing, accounting, and other matters of internal control. As a result, the hospital's financial condition had been declining until the last fiscal period when expenses exceeded revenue. Moreover, the current working capital position of the hospital was becoming critical as it became more and more difficult for Dr. Walsh to pay creditors.

At the suggestion of Dr. James, who had a bachelor's degree

in business administration, Dr. Walsh hired a hospital consultant to assist him in getting at the cause of the increase in the hospital's costs.

The consultant's analysis disclosed that (1) food costs were excessively high in relation to revenue and to other hospital costs, (2) food and linens were being stolen, probably by some employees, (3) discounts available on purchases were being lost, (4) the same few suppliers were being used, with no attention being given to alternate suppliers, (5) immediate reduction of costs was imperative if the hospital were to remain operative on a financial basis, (6) immediate relief from a very tight working

Exhibit I

THE SOUTH SHORE HOSPITAL
BALANCE SHEET
DECEMBER 31, 1957

ASSETS

Current Assets:

Cash	$ 1,521.65	
Accounts Receivable (Patients)	4,500.13	
Inventories	6,954.02	
Total Current Assets		$12,975.80

Fixed Assets:

Land		$ 1,200.00	
Building	$30,000.00		
Less Reserve for Depreciation	15,000.00	15,000.00	
Equipment	$20,000.00		
Less Reserve for Depreciation	15,000.00	5,000.00	
Total Fixed Assets			21,200.00
Total Assets			$34,175.80

LIABILITIES

Current Liabilities:

Accounts Payable	$10,500.00	
Salaries Payable	1,750.00	
Total Current Liabilities		$12,250.00

CAPITAL

M. Walsh, Capital	21,925.80
Total Liabilities and Capital	$34,175.80

capital position must be obtained if the hospital is to meet its debts as they mature (Exhibit I), (7) a new accounting system based upon sound hospital accounting principles must be installed.

Following the advice of the hospital consultant, Dr. Walsh had a simple inventory control system installed, spent a great deal more time considering alternate suppliers for food and other items that were purchased, and made every effort possible to keep internal costs down to the barest minimum. These admirable practices, of course, did not help solve the urgent problem of meeting the current debts which were already on the books before the consultant was hired. In this connection, since the hospital had no outside endowment and derived virtually all of its revenue from patient services, Dr. Walsh called Dr. James into his office to discuss this important matter.

X. AUTOMOBILE MANUFACTURERS ASSOCIATION

EVEN before Pearl Harbor, America's plants were producing a substantial volume of defense materials. Factories were working at near-peak levels turning out civilian and military products, resulting in an extraordinary demand for materials — especially steel. Because of this demand, the steel mills were finding it increasingly difficult to obtain the necessary scrap metal to sustain production. Programs were undertaken by the steel companies, and later by the government, to encourage everyone to clean up their homes, farms, and factories in order to increase the flow of scrap metal.

When the United States entered the war, still greater demands were placed on the steel industry, and the scrap shortage became even more serious. Because of the concern of nearly everyone in the nation about this problem, a situation developed which affected the automobile manufacturing industry in a special way. With passenger-car assembly lines shut down and converted to the production of war material, special machinery, tools, and dies used in the manufacture of passenger cars which were of no use in the production of military items were moved into storage yards near the plants. To the average person this equipment appeared to be junk. Questions were asked by many — including a number of nationally prominent citizens — as to why the industry did not send this apparently useless material to the steel mills to help relieve the scrap shortage. As the scrap situation continued to grow worse, government defense officials began to talk about issuing orders requiring the automobile companies to scrap these items. Extensive discussion of this matter in the press was responsible for a widespread critical public attitude toward the automobile industry.

There appeared to be several ways in which the industry might have handled the situation. The industry could have resisted all pressure to scrap the 1942 model tools and dies. This position could have been defended by putting forth several compelling

155

reasons for not scrapping the equipment. The tools and dies would be needed at the end of the war to resume civilian production quickly. Prolonged unemployment during the reconversion period would thus be avoided. In addition, the investment involved in this equipment was very large and scrapping it would mean important financial losses to the automobile companies. Finally, some of the tools and dies were needed to produce functional replacement parts necessary to maintain essential transportation during the period when no new vehicles were being produced.

But this negative attitude would have had serious results. The bad public-relations position of the industry would continue to exist and probably get worse. Furthermore, there was no assurance that the government would not adopt regulations requiring the scrapping of the equipment. Such regulations might have been so severe that the industry could have lost much more than it would under some other possible solution that could be worked out.

At the other extreme, the industry could have decided to scrap all the tools and dies. This action would have changed public attitudes toward the automobile industry from unfavorable to favorable. It would also make a substantial contribution to the scrap stockpiles. Moreover, this alternative would mean that the postwar reconversion period would be longer and unemployment greater. The automobile companies would also have to bear the loss of their investment in the facilities that were scrapped.

The Automotive Council for War Production, chiefly staffed by personnel from the Automobile Manufacturers Association, was a wartime association of vehicle and parts' manufacturers formed to work together and with defense officials to bring about maximum efficiency in the industry's war effort. The Board of Directors of the Automotive Council for War Production established a Salvage and Conservation Committee which was directed to develop programs for helping to relieve the scrap shortage.

XI. THE HAYASHI TRUST & BANKING CO., LTD.

SANZAI FUJITA, president of the Hayashi Trust & Banking Company, made the following statement in 1958:

> In spite of a recession in the world economy, the Japanese economy has enjoyed a fairly good prosperity. Savings in all banks in Japan increased 432 billion yen[1] over the last fiscal year. On the other hand, loans of all banks increased 382 billion yen since demand from the basic industries such as steel, electricity and coal has been brisk.

> Our company has grown and prospered during this time with the result that the balance of loan trust accounts is 58 billion yen (4 billion increase), money trust accounts have a balance of 20 billion yen, banking accounts have 35 billion, with a total balance of 113 billion yen, a 12 billion yen increase over the last fiscal year. The total of loans is now 103 billion yen and investment is 4 billion yen. Net profit of the company is 348 million yen.

ORIGINAL HAYASHI TRUST COMPANY

The Hayashi Trust and Banking Company was established in 1924 by Umekichi Yoneyama and other leading figures of Japanese financial circles who acted as promoters under the corporate name of The Hayashi Trust Co., Ltd. The company was capitalized at Y30,000,000 as the first of this kind to be organized under the Japanese Law of Trust. Business of the company proved successful, and at one time its total various trust properties amounted to 33.4 per cent of the entire trust accounts in Japan. When other trust companies came into existence later on, the above ratio gradually dropped, but never to below 20 per cent of the total until the end of World War II.

The original lines of business carried out by the Hayashi Trust Company were those shown in Exhibit I (see p. 158). By 1934 the company had money trust which amounted to

---

[1] The yen has exchanged for 27.79 cents from 1956 through 1958 (*Federal Reserve Bulletin*, Vol. 45, No. 11, November, 1959, p. 1441).

Exhibit I

THE HAYASHI TRUST COMPANY LINES OF BUSINESS

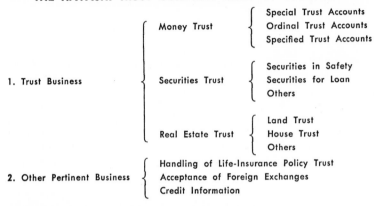

1. Trust Business	Money Trust	Special Trust Accounts / Ordinal Trust Accounts / Specified Trust Accounts
	Securities Trust	Securities in Safety / Securities for Loan / Others
	Real Estate Trust	Land Trust / House Trust / Others
2. Other Pertinent Business		Handling of Life-Insurance Policy Trust / Acceptance of Foreign Exchanges / Credit Information

17 million yen. Investment of the trust accounts was not successful because of overinvestment of the economy and the entrance of other large financial groups into the trust business. Therefore, competition became very keen.

The Hayashi Trust Company was a member of the six largest financial groups in Japan known as the Zaibatsu.[2] The six groups are called Hayashi, Sumitomo, Mitsubishi, Yasuda, Daiichi, and Nippon. The Hayashi financial group or Hayashi Zaibatsu is the largest among these groups. Each Zaibatsu has banking, mining, shipbuilding, chemical, textile, and other business interests. The position of the Zaibatsu in Japanese industries is extremely important, since the Japanese economy has been practically controlled by the Zaibatsu in an oligopolistic fashion with its few producers, many buyers, and slight price competition.

The presidents of the company during the first period of original establishment were Umekichi Yoneyama (1924–1934), Tokuzo Eto (1934–1935), Seihin Ikeda (1935–1936). The Hayashi Trust Company started with 74 employees and 19 officers. In 1936, employees increased to 281 with 18 officers. The organization consisted of the following departments: general office, accounting, trust, loan, securities, real estate, custody, and law. The company also had a branch in Osaka, the second largest city in Japan.

---

[2] The Zaibatsu are known as the great industrial families of Japan.

From the beginning, the Hayashi Trust Company made remarkable progress if we observe the increase in trust accounts during the first period (1924–1936): 1925 — 100,000,000 yen, 1928 — 300,000,000 yen, 1930 — 400,000,000 yen, and 1936 — 500,000,000 yen.

The profit of the company was mostly derived from the margin of interest charged on loans over interest paid to depositors. The average dividend paid to ordinal money trust in 1931 was 4.1 per cent and the rate of interest charged for loans was 6.35 per cent; therefore the margin was 2.25 per cent, which was comparably high. The banking business usually made something like 1.9 per cent as margin and general insurance companies made 1.6 per cent. The above-average margin was largely due to the fact that the Hayashi Trust Company was under the Hayashi Zaibatsu which controlled some 40 per cent of the industries. The Hayashi Imports and Exports Company had substantial business both in domestic and oversea markets. In almost every large country the Hayashi Imports and Exports had overseas branches, and practically 80 per cent of the Japanese international trade was carried by them. Naturally, the Hayashi Trust Company along with the Hayashi Bank supplied the necessary capital for the Hayashi Imports and Exports Company.

In Japan, financial institutions such as banks and trust companies have played an important role in economic development. In any industry, good relationships with banks or trust companies is fundamental and managers in firms are fully aware of this fact. Usually, banks will supply short-term loans and trust companies will supply long-term loans to industry. Financial institutions thus acquired power and controlled industries. Good relations with banks became the key to success in business. This was particularly true in Japan, because the Japanese economy suffers from the lack of capital, and whoever has the capital can control the industries.

WARTIME OPERATION (1937–1945)

Before the Japan-China war in 1937, the Hayashi Trust Company secured an enviable position in the financial world. In 1937, the total amount of trust accounts was over 500 million yen. During wartime, especially in 1944, the increase in the total amount of trust accounts was 80 million yen over the previous year and in 1945 the total amount was over one billion. This rapid increase was largely attributable to the government policy of encouraged savings for the wartime need. Besides, new lines of business were open. Retirement trusts and pension trusts were now available. Moreover, another development during this period was the increase in the number of new branches.

The company's investment policy was still the same as in previous years, namely, emphasis was placed upon loans rather than upon investment in stocks and securities. In 1945, 60 per cent of the investment was made in loans and 40 per cent in securities.

During the war, the company acquired the position of taking care of "enemy property," and many employees were sent to occupied territories such as China and Manchuria. Thus the company could get large amounts of savings which were almost fixed forever since the people in enemy countries were not allowed to take any property from Japan.

Problems during wartime operations included the lack of employees. Young men were drafted and therefore women had to replace them. There was some confusion about this replacement. When men were replaced by women, the women were reluctant to assume responsibility. In addition, lack of communication during and after the bombings resulted in complications.

PERIOD OF TRANSITION (1945–1948)

Runaway inflation after the war kept the total amount in the trust accounts of the six trust companies from increasing very much. In 1945, the total amount was 4,400 million yen but in 1948 it only increased to 5,300 million yen. Trust companies tried to increase savings by means of new types of trust-saving devices, but the result was not as good as they had expected. Under the inflationary shock, the Hayashi Trust Company experienced severe distress. Since the Hayashi Trust Company was virtually supported by the Hayashi Zaibatsu, and since the first thing the American government did was to separate and destroy the Zaibatsu families, the Hayashi Zaibatsu was also destroyed. The result was a significant decrease in the company's profits.

One of the most important events during this period was the changing of the six major trust companies in Japan to trust and "banking" companies. Because of the severe inflation after the war, trust companies could not maintain their position as long-term money suppliers in the financial world. The long-term savings were the first hit by the inflation. It thus became a matter of emergency to carry on some other business in addition to trust operations. The banking business saved the trust companies. In 1948, the company, together with other trust companies in Japan, was authorized to engage in the banking business and commenced to handle bank deposits and other banking operations. The capital of the company was increased to 50 million yen. This changeover increased competition, since the company had to compete with the former Hayashi Bank, now Taikoku Bank.

PERIOD OF TRUST AND BANKING OPERATION (1948–THE PRESENT)

The result of operating the banking business was very favorable to the company. At the end of 1948 the total amount of such business was 400 million yen, and at the end of 1949 it amounted to 3,400 million yen. Money-trust accounts also showed a slight increase. In 1948 the balance was 1,000 million yen and it increased to 10 billion yen in 1952. The percentage of money-trust accounts decreased, however, due to the rapid increase in the other accounts.

With the banking business there came several problems which management had to solve. One was whether or not the company should give up its trust business. Trust business was very successful before the war when the economy was stable. Now the managers suspected that the cost of management of the trust accounts was so high that it was not worthwhile maintaining the accounts. After considerable discussion, the company decided to maintain the trust accounts, although emphasis should now be placed upon the banking business.

Although the company was successful in engaging in the banking business, management had to solve the important problem arising from branch offices. So long as they engaged in the trust business the number of branches was not significant to the company's business. But banking operations presupposed as many branches as possible. Without branches the company could not compete with other banks. Government policy, however, of not allowing the trust companies to establish as many branches as they needed was reflected in the opinion that this would lead to severe competition among banks and trust companies.

In 1950 the company merged with the Nihon Investment Trust Co., Ltd. Subsequently, the capital of the company gradually increased and reached Y300,000,000 in 1952.

By the end of the Korean War the company had established its postwar foundation in both the trust and banking operations. New lines of trust operations were brought into the company's business. One was the "investment trust" in 1951. The other was the "loan trust" in 1952. The role of the investment trust in trust companies was secondary, since the trust companies handled office work for securities companies who were depositing a part of the money they collected from the customers. In other words, the securities company receives money by selling investment trust certificates. The securities company then request the Hayashi Trust and Banking Company to do the office work for which the company received nothing but a small commission for the services rendered.

The loan trust was a really new device and saved the trust companies from an inferior position because of the keen competition in the financial business. In 1952, the government passed the Law of Loan Trust to enable trust companies to engage in loan trust. The six major Zaibatsu trust companies were allowed to do the business. The trust companies sell loan-trust certificates and receive the money in trust. The terms were for two and five years. One unit of loan trust is Y5,000 and ordinarily customers buy ten units which amount to Y50,000. The customers receive a dividend of 6 per cent for a two-year loan trust and 8 per cent for a five-year loan trust. The company can then loan the money to basic industries specified by the law, such as the electric, steel, coal, shipbuilding, and other related industries. The company loans at a 10–12 per cent rate of interest depending upon the nature of the loans and the condition of the companies concerned.

ORGANIZATION AT THE PRESENT TIME

The organization chart of the company is shown in Exhibit II.

ORGANIZATION CHART OF   Exhibit II
THE HAYASHI TRUST AND BANKING CO.*

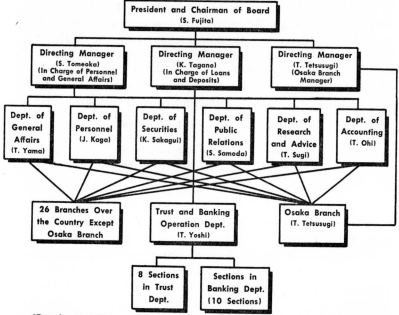

*December 31, 1957.

The president of the company, S. Fujita is a very mild-mannered person. Although he is very enthusiastic in his work, he never shows his real power. He entered the company on its establishment, after graduating from Tokyo Imperial University. He usually does not go into detail but delegates a great deal of his authority to other directing managers, especially to S. Tomeoka who is in charge of a large number of departments and virtually runs the company.

Another directing manager, Mr. K. Tagano, is a specialist in the loan business. He decides the companies to which the firm will lend money and how much should be loaned.

Mr. T. Tetsusugi is in charge of the trust department. He is younger than any of the foregoing and is manager of the largest branch of Osaka. The dual position of Mr. Tetsusugi in the hierarchy is indicative of some overlapping of authority and responsibility resulting from poor job definitions (see Exhibit II).

LOAN-TRUST OPERATION

When the loan trust was put into operation, it was clear that it would appeal to the ordinary middle-class families since the dividend was so high. When the trust was extended into the loan trust in 1952 the first collection amounted to 600 million yen. Since then it increased rapidly, and in 1958 it amounted to 58 billion yen with the ratio of loan trust to total deposits now almost 50 per cent. The increase in loan-trust accounts is shown by presenting the balance at the end of each year since 1952:

1952	1.2 billion yen
1953	11.8 billion yen
1954	12.0 billion yen
1955	18.3 billion yen
1956	25.1 billion yen
1957	40.3 billion yen
1958	58.4 billion yen

Other trust and banking companies are also trying to increase their loan-trust accounts. The Sumitomo Trust and Banking Company has been on top since the war in every field, and this is also true for the loan-trust accounts. The Hayashi Trust and Banking Company was second in the amount of loan-trust accounts.

The dividend varies according to general economic conditions and revenue made by the company by lending loan trust to industries. Six large trust and banking companies have an agreement to pay the same rate of dividend approved by the government. Average rates are such that a two-year loan trust paid 8.1 per cent and a five-year paid 9.1 per cent in 1954. In 1958, the two-year rate was 7.5 per cent and the five-year was 8.8 per cent.

COMPETITIVE CONDITIONS

As noted earlier, the Hayashi Trust & Banking Company used to be first among the trust business, primarily because it was the first one of its kind. Since the war greatly damaged the Hayashi Zaibatsu, it is safe to say that this is one of the reasons why the company became second or third.

The Hayashi people are still dreaming of the good old days. Their problem seems to be that someone, especially the Sumitomo, steals their ideas and puts them into practice earlier. This was true when the loan trust was first introduced. The Hayashi is too conservative and their business philosophy is obsolete. They used to be asked to do business instead of doing the asking. They are passive and impractical.

Differences in management are also clearly evident between the Hayashi and the Mitsubishi. The Mitsubishi has a tradition like the Hayashi, but they realize that times are changing and innovations are necessary to improve and make more

Exhibit III

BALANCE OF MONEY TRUST, LOAN TRUST, AND DEPOSITS*
(THE HAYASHI TRUST & BANKING CO.)

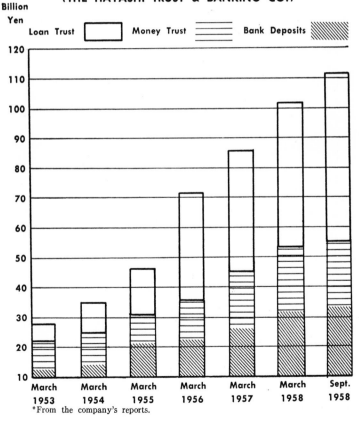

Loan Trust   Money Trust   Bank Deposits

Billion Yen

*From the company's reports.

Exhibit IV

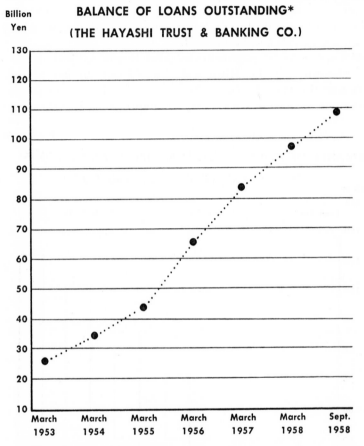

Billion Yen

BALANCE OF LOANS OUTSTANDING*
(THE HAYASHI TRUST & BANKING CO.)

*From the company's reports.

money. On the other hand, the Hayashi respects tradition and the old way. For example, about three years ago most of the Japanese firms and banks were introducing I.B.M. equipment. The Mitsubishi immediately decided to use I.B.M. When the Hayashi heard of this, one of the managers said, "The Mitsubishi is throwing money away for that kind of thing." But in two years, the Hayashi was obliged to introduce I.B.M. because of the competition.

Exhibit V

THE HAYASHI TRUST AND BANKING CO.
CONSOLIDATED BALANCE SHEET
1. Trust Account (Million Yen)

ASSETS	1948	1949	1950	1951	1952	1953
Cash and Due From Banks	658	775	951	1.663	2.681	2.902
Call Loans	269	380	460	489	501	706
Securities	160	171	190	170	176	298
Securities Under Trust	. . .	. . .	. . .	1.001	4.500	5.001
Bills Discounted	898	1.113	963	1.190	1.326	1.338
Loans	1.105	639	2.326	3.062	5.424	10.010
Other Assets	460	650	790	1.663	1.301	1.447
Total	3.550	3.728	5.680	9.238	15.909	20.892

ASSETS	1954	1955	1956	1957	1958*
Cash and Due From Banks	3.052	3.582	4.261	4.265	1.065
Call Loans	768	993	1.009	1.559	2.089
Securities	305	265	321	575	536
Securities Under Trust	6.334	8.001	8.059	8.065	17.744
Bills Discounted	1.501	1.606	1.961	2.126	2.824
Loans	17.736	22.378	31.030	53.018	72.420
Other Assets	1.625	1.903	2.000	2.063	6.665
Total	30.821	38.728	48.641	71.671	103.243

LIABILITIES	1948	1949	1950	1951	1952	1953
Money Trust	2.221	3.321	5.182	7.606	9.235	10.658
Loan Trust	. . .	. . .	. . .	. . .	1.203	4.231
Security Trust (Investment)	. . .	. . .	. . .	1.125	4.936	5.339
Securities in Trust	326	401	490	502	531	656
Claims in Trust	1	3	4	3	2	4
Equipment in Trust	. . .	. . .	. . .	. . .	. . .	. . .
Real Estate in Trust	2	3	4	2	2	4
Total	3.550	3.728	5.680	9.238	15.909	20.892

LIABILITIES	1954	1955	1956	1957	1958*
Money Trust	11.462	10.338	12.699	17.898	20.260
Loan Trust	11.328	18.650	25.128	41.246	58.216
Security Trust (Investment)	7.249	8.816	9.765	11.278	19.971
Securities in Trust	775	918	1.005	1.122	3.656
Claims in Trust	4	4	4	4	5
Equipment in Trust	. . .	. . .	36	117	1.133
Real Estate in Trust	3	2	4	6	2
Total	30.821	38.728	48.641	71.671	103.243

* September, 1958. All other figures are for March.

Exhibit VI

THE HAYASHI TRUST AND BANKING CO.
CONSOLIDATED BALANCE SHEET
2. Banking Account (Million Yen)

ASSETS	1948	1949	1950	1951	1952	1953
Cash and Due From Banks	2.701	2.535	3.695	4.005	4.998	5.623
Securities	646	763	871	950	1.137	1.359
Bills Discounted	683	1.088	645	735	1.651	2.713
Loans	2.481	3.530	5.687	7.231	7.712	8.822
Customers' Liability	712	972	1.621	1.874	2.174	2.353
Bank Premises	119	368	549	756	720	945
Others	270	219	315	544	315	949
Total	7.610	9.475	13.383	16.095	18.507	22.764

ASSETS	1954	1955	1956	1957	1958*	
Cash and Due From Banks	6.350	5.130	5.823	6.445	8.817	
Securities	1.358	1.321	1.528	2.921	6.291	
Bills Discounted	14.316	15.581	16.554	14.412	14.866	
Loans	4.454	5.960	4.230	12.169	17.002	
Customers' Liability	3.629	3.940	3.662	4.147	3.664	
Bank Premises	833	663	581	684	905	
Others	1.326	1.520	1.625	2.000	1.769	
Total	28.266	34.135	34.003	42.779	53.314	

LIABILITIES	1948	1949	1950	1951	1952	1953
Deposits	4.412	5.423	8.635	9.785	11.067	12.779
Borrowed Money From						
Bank of Japan	875	936	1.130	1.360	1.526	2.538
Call Money	955	1.356	1.556	2.626	2.934	3.588
Acceptance	775	907	959	1.219	1.520	1.860
Capital	100	200	200	200	300	600
Reserve	323	355	435	545	631	705
Earned Surplus	170	298	468	360	529	694
Total	7.610	9.475	13.383	16.095	18.507	22.764

LIABILITIES	1954	1955	1956	1957	1958*	
Deposits	16.985	21.533	22.681	27.456	35.122	
Borrowed Money From						
Bank of Japan	3.598	2.598	3.231	2.368	1.476	
Call Money	3.296	4.235	3.458	4.270	4.578	
Acceptance	1.987	3.262	1.650	4.509	6.664	
Capital	600	600	600	1.200	1.200	
Reserve	905	960	1.151	1.386	1.576	
Earned Surplus	895	947	1.232	1.590	2.774	
Total	28.266	34.135	34.003	42.779	53.314	

* September, 1958. All other figures are for March.

Exhibit VII

THE HAYASHI TRUST AND BANKING CO.
CONSOLIDATED INCOME STATEMENT
(In Million Yen)

ITEMS———YEAR	1948	1949	1950	1951	1952	1953
Loan Interest	390	431	325	624	584	663
Trust Revenue	298	425	485	463	363	489
Discounted Revenue	260	338	260	458	446	456
Others	96	472	314	597	516	529
Total Revenue	1.044	1.656	1.484	2.342	1.909	2.137

ITEMS———YEAR	1954	1955	1956	1957	1958*	
Loan Interest	537	663	732	865	980	
Trust Revenue	433	580	540	429	598	
Discounted Revenue	521	552	654	721	780	
Others	575	441	517	623	548	
Total Revenue	2.066	2.236	2.443	2.638	2.906	

ITEMS———YEAR	1948	1949	1950	1951	1952	1953
Deposit Interest Expense	414	532	540	599	521	716
Loan Expenses	320	460	340	758	335	519
Salaries and Wages	127	311	330	496	499	460
Others	79	225	104	597	395	297
Total Expenses	940	1.528	1.314	2.450	1.740	1.972

ITEMS———YEAR	1954	1955	1956	1957	1958*	
Deposit Interest Expense	681	760	724	860	850	
Loan Expenses	550	501	529	540	659	
Salaries and Wages	433	402	531	597	444	
Others	201	348	374	321	605	
Total Expenses	1.865	2.011	2.158	2.318	2.558	

	1948	1949	1950	1951	1952	1953
Total Revenue	1.044	1.656	1.484	2.342	1.909	2.137
Total Expenses	940	1.528	1.314	2.450	1.740	1.972
Net Profit	104	128	170	(108)	169	165

	1954	1955	1956	1957	1958*	
Total Revenue	2.066	2.236	2.443	2.638	2.906	
Total Expenses	1.865	2.011	2.158	2.318	2.558	
Net Profit	201	225	285	320	348	

* September, 1958. All other figures are for March.

XII. SOCIAL SERVICES, INC.

HISTORY

Social Services, Inc., came into existence during the summer of 1956 as the result of a merger of two Catholic social agencies which were operated and supervised for some forty years by the Catholic archdiocese of a large metropolitan area. The archdiocese felt that there would be better operating results if the two agencies were combined. By centralizing functions, better service could be administered and financial savings would result by eliminating the cost of operating the two agencies. As was the case when the two agencies were operating, the goal of the merged operation is to provide counseling and guidance to homeless children and other related cases.

The agency receives funds from the United Community Services as well as the Juvenile Court of the County. The court pays the agency a certain rate per week for each child it assigns under the jurisdiction of the agency. In the case of noncourt children, the UCS pays the agency a stipulated amount per week per child. In addition, UCS also provides the agency with funds in order to meet payrolls, operating expenses, and other miscellaneous expenses.

The rates received for each child from the court and from the UCS are paid to the various boarding homes and institutions which take care of the children which the agency assigns to them. The agency operates well over 300 boarding homes. These homes are regular family homes which have been made available for the specific purpose of providing a place for the children to stay. The family involved receives the stipulated rate from the agency each month.

In addition, the agency also sends children assigned to it to various institutions such as Father Flannagan's Boy's Town, Philadelphia Protectory, St. Francis Home for Boys, and other places conducted and operated by different religious (Catholic) orders and the archdiocese of a particular city. Generally, however, most children are placed within the metropolitan and suburban area where the agency is located.

ORGANIZATION

On the average, 100 caseworkers are employed by the agency to handle the more than 1000 children under its jurisdiction. All are qualified, and the majority have college degrees in the field of social science. The work of these social workers is supervised by district supervisors who report to the director of the agency as well as two administrative executives (see Exhibit I).

The agency has a separate department for handling unmarried mothers, child care, family service, and adoptive children. Each department has an intake supervisor who is responsible for handling a case when it is initially brought to the attention of the agency. The intake supervisor, after gathering all the necessary data concerning a particular case, will then turn the case over to the appropriate district supervisor. The district supervisor, who handles a certain section of the city, will then assign the case to a social worker for further action.

The accounting department comprises two women, Miss Smith and Miss Jones. Miss Smith is responsible for the recording of all transactions in the appropriate books of account, making bank deposits and issuing checks. Miss Jones is responsible for making out the monthly court bill, which contains all the children under the jurisdiction of the agency for which the court pays a certain weekly rate. In addition, Miss Jones also makes out the checks for the various boarding homes and institutions.

The statistical department also contains two women, Miss Brown and Miss White. The main function of this department is to prepare monthly reports to show the number of children cared for, the number of boarding homes in use, the number of institutions, etc. These reports are not only submitted to the administrative executive and director but to the UCS as well. They are useful in determining whether or not the agency has enough workers to cope with the cases, the amount of the load assigned to each caseworker, and in preparing the annual budget.

The stenographic department is supervised by Miss Black. The department is made up, on the average, of ten women who type

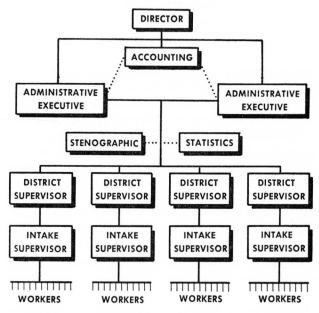

Exhibit I

SOCIAL SERVICES, INC.

ORGANIZATIONAL CHART

up the cases once they have been accepted by the agency and perform miscellaneous typing and clerical duties.

The filing department is responsible for the orderly filing of all cases under the jurisdiction of the agency. Whenever a social worker, executive, supervisor, or the director wants to obtain certain information with respect to a given case, the filing department is expected to provide this information. The department is operated by two women.

INTAKE PROCEDURE

This phase of operations deals with the handling of a case when it is initially brought to the attention of the agency.

The intake worker receives a request for service and then makes out an application slip and a temporary index card. On the temporary index card are entered the name of the client, address, date, date of appointment, and the name of the worker with whom the appointment is to be kept, code, and worker's name. The temporary index card is then placed in a designated box near the intake offices to be picked up by the clerical person.

The latter files the temporary index card in the master index file. If the case has been known previously to the agency, the file or files are pulled and given to the worker with whom the client has an appointment.

When the intake worker has completed an interview with the client, he will then dictate the information he has obtained from the client into a dictaphone machine. The worker, when dictating, will indicate that the case is to be made up into a folder for continued service, that the case may be a brief service, or that the dictation should be returned to him with the application slip, pending further action.

When the case is to be made up into a folder, the designated clerical person checks again in the agency master index file, having the benefit of additional information, such as previous marriages, aliases, etc.

The case is entered in a register and a number is given. If the case is to be reopened, the name is entered in the register and the old number is used. The register contains the following items: date, number, name of client, source of referral, request by code, parish of residence of the client.

The master index card is then made out. This includes the name of the client (surname and given names of husband and wife, or, if an unmarried mother, the first name of the client), children's names, worker's name, case number, and date of opening of case.

A fact sheet is filled out and placed in the folder along with the dictation. A statistical card is typed out and attached to the front of the case, and then a label is put on the folder giving number, surname, man's and woman's given names.

The case is now open to the intake worker whose name is written in pencil on the master index card. The case is returned by the typist to the intake worker, who in turn transfers it to the intake supervisor. The intake supervisor then sends the case and statistical card on to the district supervisor. The intake supervisor sends a "Statistical Change" or "Assignment Within the Month" form to the clerical department where the district supervisor's name is entered in pencil on the master index card.

The district supervisor assigns the case to a worker, giving the case to the worker and sending the statistical card and "Notice of Statistical Change" or "Assignment Within the Month" through to the clerical department, where the continuing worker's name is entered on the master index card.

The above intake procedures are generally applicable to all departments of the agency.

However, with respect to child-care intake, certain other procedures are followed. The child-care worker will accept the following types of requests for placement: referrals from the juvenile court when that agency is active on a case, referrals from the public agencies when they are active, referrals from other casework agencies, and referrals which occasionally might come from outside the regular area of service.

Social Services, Inc., has known from day-by-day experience that one of the great gaps in casework service to children needing care outside of their own homes is the lack of establishing initial relationships with them and preparing them for placement. Cases of this type were not assigned from intake to the district worker until the boarding home had been found for the child. This meant that usually no one saw the child until the point of placement, or very shortly before this. The agency had insufficient knowledge of the child, and the child frequently had no knowledge of what was happening to him.

As a result of the above situation, the functions of the child-care intake worker are now as follows:

1. If the case situation so indicates, she will do a more complete diagnostic study than may have already been done, to define need for placement as well as the fact that the child falls within the program of the agency.

2. She will, whenever possible, have contacts with the child in terms of getting to know him, determining what type of care will best meet his needs, and prepare him for coming in for agency care. In some cases where there is urgent need for placement this might not be possible, but it should be attempted in every case in which it can be done. This will involve outside work

for the intake worker who will be visiting the child in his own home, the detention home, etc.

3. When the diagnostic decision is made, the intake department will then have to seek the indicated resources for placement within the agency.

4. The intake worker will have contact with parents, when possible, to interpret the foster-care program to them, to develop an initial relationship with the agency, and to have the medical consents and financial arrangements (in cases of voluntary placements) signed.

5. At the point at which the placement facility is determined the case will move from the intake department for assignment to the ongoing worker.

In moving the case from the intake department to the child-care worker, the intake supervisor will give the case record and statistical card with the assignment or transfer directly to the administrative supervisor of the child-care division who will make the assignment to the proper worker. She will send the assignment or transfer slip with the statistical card to the stenographic department and forward the record to the worker.

After the family or child-care intake worker has arrived at a decision that placement is necessary or indicated, a request is made to the placement co-ordinator for the proper placement, either institutional or boarding care. The caseworker needs to describe to the co-ordinator the type of child and the kind of facility needed so that the co-ordinator can select the proper resource. If this is a boarding home the co-ordinator will see to it that the proper contact is made with the, boarding parents to see whether they will accept this child. If the facility is an institution the co-ordinator contacts the home to make arrangements with the administrator.

In the meantime, the worker prepares the child and family for placement. She obtains the signatures on the medical agreement, financial agreement, and any other forms required, and secures baptismal records. When all is ready the worker attempts, whenever possible, to introduce the family to the child-care worker who will be responsible for making the placement. In general the case will be transferred to the child-care worker, but after interdivision consultation, it may be retained by the family worker if she is to remain active on the case for further family counseling.

CASEWORKER'S WORK SHEETS

The caseworker's work sheet is used by the individual caseworker to list his case load and to record activity on and status of each case. Three work sheets are used: (1) Form 8A is designed for case workers who carry no responsibility for home finding; (2) Form 9A is designed for case workers whose responsibilities are confined to home finding, and (3) Form 8A-9A is intended for caseworkers who carry a regular case load as well as home finding.

Form 8A covers service to families and to children, whether served in the homes of their own parents or elsewhere. Cases are listed according to the family name, with the names of children served outside the homes of their own parents indented immediately below the case name. For each child receiving service, a family unit is listed, but no family unit should be listed more than once regardless of the number of members served or the number of services given. These lists comprise the over-all case count for the agency in terms of family units, and also provide the count of children served outside their parents' homes.

Form 9A is concerned with applications to provide foster or adoptive care, study of such applications, and use of foster and adoptive homes by the agency. Because of differences in agency allocation of responsibility for work on foster homes and differences in agency bookkeeping procedures, some flexibility is assumed in the use of this work sheet.

When the forms used by the caseworkers were discussed with Miss Blue, one of the administrative executives, she noted that the forms were rather large and complex and represented quite a project for the caseworker. These forms are used in compiling statistics for scrutiny by the administrative executives, supervisors, and director. "In view of the complexity and number of forms, case workers seldom turn in their forms on time," she said. "These forms should be in the hands of the statistical unit about ten days after the end of each month, but rarely are. By the time the statistical unit completes the compilation of the information, the finished report usually finds its way to my desk well after the fifteenth of the month." In conclusion, she stated: "The reports lose quite a bit of their value when they are handed in so late. We certainly would like to find a way whereby these reports would be turned in on time."

ACCOUNTING

Theoretically, the accounting department should consist of a general accountant, assistant accountant, and boarding-home clerk. However, at the present time only Miss Smith and Miss Jones are handling the bulk of the accounting work.

Under the theoretical plan, the general accountant should be in charge of all accounts and records of the organization with responsibility to the director. He maintains the accounts in accordance with UCS requirements and follows good accounting practices customarily followed by similar organizations.

The duties of the general accountant and his assistant are:

1. Receive all cash receipts of the agency including checks or currency either received by mail or in the office.

2. Promptly record such receipts in the cash-receipts book which shall clearly show the source and the type of receipt classified into such columnar form as will permit easy posting of the general ledger.

3. Deposit all receipts promptly to the credit of the agency in the proper accounts.

4. Prepare all checks and record in the check register the date, check number, amount, and account distribution in such columnar form as will permit easy posting of the general ledger.

5. Require proper authority before issuing any check and retain such authorization in the files.

6. Maintain a petty-cash fund under the imprest system and a reasonable amount to be determined by the director and reimburse the fund as necessary.

7. Maintain attendance records necessary to the proper preparation of payrolls. Prepare semimonthly payrolls, summaries, and earnings records for all persons in the employ. Make all necessary and proper deductions and maintain proper records relating thereto. Prepare and file all necessary tax reports in connection with the payroll.

8. Maintain the general journal and make necessary entries during the course of the year. Maintain the general ledger in such form that the UCS budget report can be prepared directly from the ledger. Post from the books of original entry to the ledger. Take a trial balance monthly and insure that the ledger is in balance. Reconcile all bank accounts.

9. Prepare the UCS budget report monthly and see that it is signed and submitted within a reasonable time. Prepare and submit all bills to the county courts and other public agencies and maintain proper records in order to insure that the agency is duly reimbursed. Also, where necessary, send invoices or statements to other agencies or parents for amounts due to the agency. In this regard, particular care should be exercised to account for the number of days of care provided in every boarding home or institution.

10. Maintain records to support disbursements to the boarding-home parents. Prepare and mail these checks monthly by the fifteenth of the month.

11. Special reports or analysis required by the director from time to time should be prepared and where necessary other personnel of the agency may be drawn on to give assistance.

"The above duties look very good, but they are not being carried out as they should," Miss Smith pointed out. "There is too much work for two people to handle. Also, the files we have with respect to boarding homes and children in care are cumbersome and not completely accurate," she added. "There seems to be no harmony or smooth flow of work. Everybody seems to be going around in circles."

It was found out that Miss Smith is a complainer by nature. She is a good worker, but likes to make her gripes known constantly. Miss Jones, on the other hand, is unassuming and seldom complains. She does her work and gets it out, although rarely on time.

The auditor in charge of the agency account hired a young college man to assist in the accounting department. However, the latter can only devote several hours a day to the department. These hours are usually spent in making out the monthly budget, closing the general ledger for the month, and other incidental duties which take up most of his time. As a result he cannot render much help to the two girls who have to do the bulk of the work. Hence, the reason for complaints and overloading of work.

STATISTICS

This department is concerned mainly with the preparation of monthly reports regarding case loads, number of boarding homes, number of children in care, and other information. Most of this information is derived from the reports that workers turn in at the end of each month.

It was learned that Miss White and Miss Brown are quite capable to handle the job of statistics. However, because of the lateness of the reports turned in by the caseworkers, the statisticians cannot compile the necessary reports in time to reach the administrative executive's desk by the tenth of the following month.

"If the workers would only turn in the reports on time, we could do a much better job of getting information out on time," Miss White noted. "We are completely powerless to do anything about the situation and no one else really seems to care. It's strictly a hit or miss situation."

Miss Brown noted that one of the most important forms used by the worker is the "BH#1" — Notice of Placement and/or Financial Arrangements. "This form is extremely important because it tells of any changes or transfers of children from one boarding home or institution to another. It also notes any new children or boarding homes accepted," she pointed out. "This information is extremely valuable to us as well as the accounting department. The form should be turned in not later than fortyeight hours after the change or transfer has taken place. The general tendency is to turn them in late, sometimes as much as a month late, and as a result we cannot compile accurate statistics, let alone get them out on time."

STENOGRAPHIC AND CLERICAL

This department is supervised by Miss Black, a rather capable individual who can get the work out. She was recently given an assistant. The department, in general, comprises ten stenographers and typists. Their duties center mainly on the preparation of cases. The intake worker sends the stenographic department the tape from the dictaphone and it is transcribed and the necessary information typed and recorded in a case folder. In addition, miscellaneous typing and general office work is carried on by this department.

The department also operates a rather large addressograph machine. This machine is used for the sole purpose of putting names of children on the court bill which is prepared by the accounting department. "It seems like a lot of waste of machinery," Miss Black pointed out. "We use it once a month and that's it."

FILING

The filing department is operated by two girls. Whenever a case worker wants a particular case folder, he obtains it through this department. There is no centralized filing; that is, quite a few files are spread out over the confines of the administrative offices. Many of the files contain old records and many of the current records are not up to date. These observations were made by Miss Black as well as the two girls in the department.

APPENDIX

THE VALUE PROBLEM

An Economic Approach

THE selection or choice of one from among several alternatives implies a process of evaluation, that is, a process of determining preferences among the consequences of alternatives. To each alternative corresponds a unique set of related consequences. The decision-maker, in his appraisal, weighs and considers the values involved. In this connection, the economists have developed a conceptual model[1] for describing this process — known as the indifference curve.[2] In terms of the indifference curve approach, the decisions of an individual among competing values may be described by a system of indifference curves. These indifference curves indicate which sets of consequences of alternatives are equivalent to each other or indifferent on a value basis, as well as those which are preferred. That is, it is a matter of indifference to the decision-maker as to which set of consequences, and consequently alternatives, he chooses on a given indifference curve, such as curve AA in the illustration on p. 182 because he would just as soon have Y_1P_1 of X values plus P_1X_1 of Y values for alternative 1 as Y_2P_2 of X values plus P_2X_2 of Y values for alternative 2, whereas the decision-maker would definitely prefer the sets of consequences of alternatives which lie along a higher indifference curve, such as BB which would give him Y_3P_3 of X values plus P_3X_3 of Y values for alternative 3, or better yet, curve CC, which would give him Y_4P_4 of X values plus P_4X_4 of Y values for alternative 4, because BB contains a more desirable system of values than AA, while CC contains a more desirable system of values than BB, and so on.

Certain limitations are necessarily introduced in the indifference curve analysis. It is assumed that the decision-maker starts

---

[1] A model is an approximation of reality.

[2] For a complete discussion of this subject, see George J. Stigler, *The Theory of Price* (New York: The Macmillan Co., 1946), Chap. 5.

with given value preferences, that the decision-maker can substitute one alternative for another, and that he attempts to maximize his value preferences. Moreover, the values of any personal behavior system are highly individualized and volatile due to changes in space, time, and individual proclivities. Finally, only two value variables can be examined on a two-dimensional

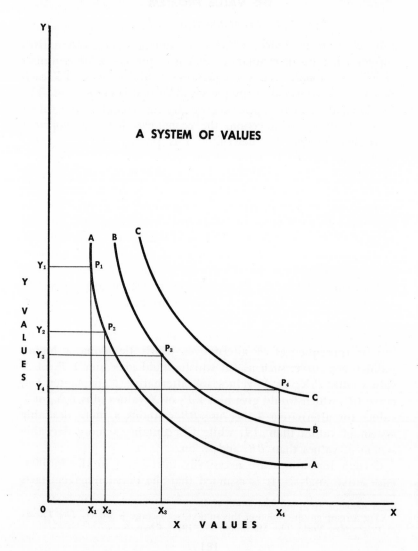

A SYSTEM OF VALUES

diagram whereas decision-making situations may involve many variables. Nevertheless, such limitations are no argument against the validity of the concept; the practical utilization of the concept can, however, be only approximate and is made somewhat difficult because of the limitations of the analysis.

BIBLIOGRAPHY

BOOKS

Ambrose, A., and Laserowitz, M., *Fundamentals of Symbolic Logic*. New York: Rinehart & Co., Inc., 1948.

Bachhuber, Andrew H., S.J., *Introduction to Logic*. New York: Appleton-Century-Crofts, Inc., 1957.

Barnard, Chester I., *The Function of the Executive*. Cambridge: Harvard University Press, 1938.

Bellman, Richard, *Dynamic Programming*. Princeton: Princeton University Press, 1957.

Bender, James F., *Technique of Executive Leadership*. New York: McGraw-Hill Book Co., 1950.

Bernhardt, Karl S., *Practical Psychology*. New York: McGraw-Hill Book Co., 1945.

Bittle, Celestine N., *The Science of Correct Thinking*. Milwaukee: The Bruce Publishing Co., 1935.

Blackwell, David, and Girshick, M. A., *Theory of Games and Statistical Decisions*. New York: John Wiley & Sons, Inc., 1954.

Blanshard, Brand, *The Nature of Thought*, Vol. II. London: George Allen & Unwin, Ltd., 1939.

Boaz, Franz, *Anthropology and Modern Life,* rev. ed. New York: W. W. Norton & Co., Inc., 1928.

Bogardus, Emory S., *Fundamentals of Social Psychology*, 4th ed. New York: Appleton-Century-Crofts, Inc., 1950.

Boulding, K. E., *Economic Analysis,* rev. ed. New York: Harper & Brothers, Publishers, 1948.

Bourke, Vernon J., *Ethics*. New York: The Macmillan Co., 1944.

Bross, Irwin D. J., *Design for Decision*. New York: The Macmillan Company, 1953.

Burtt, Edwin Arthur, *Right Thinking*, 3rd ed. New York: Harper & Brothers, 1946.

Carnap, Rudolf, *The Nature and Application of Inductive Logic*. Chicago: The University of Chicago Press, 1950.

Churchman, C. W., Ackoff, R. L., and Arnoff, E. L., *Introduction to Operations Research.* New York: John Wiley & Sons, Inc., 1957.

Cohen, Morris R., and Nagel, Ernest, *An Introduction to Logic and Scientific Method.* New York: Harcourt, Brace & Co., 1934.

Cordnier, R. J., *New Frontiers for Professional Managers.* New York: McGraw-Hill Book Co., 1956.

Cronbach, Lee J., and Gleser, Goldine C., *Psychological Tests and Personal Decisions.* Urbana: University of Illinois Press, 1957.

Davidson, D., Suppes, P., and Siegel, S., *Decision-Making: An Experimental Approach.* Stanford: Stanford University Press, 1957.

Davis, Ralph Currier, *The Fundamentals of Top Management.* New York: Harper & Brothers, 1951.

Dean, Joel, *Managerial Economics.* New York: Prentice-Hall, Inc., 1951.

Devine, Carl T., *Cost Accounting and Analysis.* New York: The Macmillan Co., 1950.

Dewey, John, *Logic, The Theory of Inquiry.* New York: Henry Holt & Co., 1938.

Drucher, Peter F., *The Concept of the Corporation.* New York: The John Day Co., 1946.

——— *The Practice of Management.* New York: Harper & Brothers, Publishers, 1954.

Dubin, Robert, *Human Relations in Administration.* New York: Prentice-Hall, Inc., 1951.

Duddy, Edward A., and Revzan, David A., *Marketing.* New York: McGraw-Hill Book Co., 1947.

Fortune, By the Editors of, *The Executive Life.* Garden City, New York: Doubleday & Co., Inc., 1956.

Glover, John G., *Business Operational Research and Reports.* New York: American Book Co., 1949.

Gordon, Robert Aaron, *Business Leadership in the Large Corporation.* Washington, D. C.: The Brookings Institution, 1945.

Harmon, Francis Lelande, *Principles of Psychology,* rev. ed. Milwaukee: The Bruce Publishing Co., 1951.

Hershovitz, Melville J., *Man and His Works*. New York: Alfred A. Knopf, 1948.

Holden, Paul E., Fish, Lounsbury S., and Smith, Hubert L., *Top-Management Organization and Control*. Stanford: Stanford University Press, 1948.

Humphrey, George, *Thinking, An Introduction to Its Experimental Psychology*. New York: John Wiley & Sons, Inc., 1951.

Jamison, Charles L., *Business Policy*. New York: Prentice-Hall, Inc., 1953.

Joad, C. E. M., *How Our Minds Work*. New York: Philosophical Library, 1947.

Jones, M. H., *Executive Decision-Making*. Homewood: Richard D. Irwin, Inc., 1957.

Katona, George, *Psychological Analysis of Economic Behavior*, 1st ed. New York: McGraw-Hill Book Co., Inc., 1951.

Kreyche, Robert J., *Logic for Undergraduates*. New York: The Dryden Press, Inc., 1954.

Laird, Donald A., and Laird, Eleanor C., *Practical Business Psychology*. New York: The Gregg Publishing Co., 1951.

Laslett, Peter (ed.), *The Physical Basis of Mind*. Oxford: Basil Blackwell, 1950.

Learned, Edmund P., Ulrich, David N., and Booz, Donald R., *Executive Action*. Boston: Harvard University, 1951.

Leys, Wayne A. R., *Ethics for Policy Decisions*. New York: Prentice-Hall, 1952.

Lindworsky, Johannes, *The Psychology of Asceticism*. St. Louis: B. Herder Book Co., 1935.

—— *Training of the Will*. Milwaukee: The Bruce Publishing Co., 1929.

Luce, Duncan, and Raiffa, Howard, *Games and Decisions: Introduction and Critical Survey*. New York: John Wiley & Sons, Inc., 1957.

Maier, Norman R. F., *Principles of Human Relations*. New York: John Wiley & Sons, Inc., 1952.

Maritain, Jacques, *An Introduction to Philosophy,* translated by E. I. Watkin. New York: Sheed & Ward, Inc., 1937.

—— *Formal Logic*. New York: Sheed & Ward, Inc., 1946.

Maziarz, Edward A., C.PP.S., *The Philosophy of Mathematics.* New York: Philosophical Library, 1950.

Meyer, John R., and Kuh, Edwin, *The Investment Decision: An Empirical Study.* Cambridge: Harvard University Press, 1957.

Mill, John Stuart, *A System of Logic,* 10th ed., Vol. I. London: Longmans, Green & Co., 1879.

Miltner, Charles C., *The Elements of Ethics,* 2nd rev. ed. New York: The Macmillan Co., 1936.

Murray, Raymond W., *Introductory Sociology.* New York: Appleton-Century-Crofts., Inc., 1946.

Newman, William H., *Administrative Action.* New York: Prentice-Hall, Inc., 1951.

Northrop, F. S. C., *The Logic of the Sciences and the Humanities.* New York: The Macmillan Co., 1947.

Owens, Richard N., *Introduction to Business Policy.* Homewood: Richard D. Irwin, Inc., 1954.

Paton, W. A., *Advanced Accounting.* New York: The Macmillan Co., 1941.

Reilly, William, *Straight Thinking,* 4th ed. New York: Harper & Brothers, 1935.

Ricciardi, Franc M., and others, *Top Management Decision Simulation.* New York: American Management Association, 1958.

Ross, W. D., *Aristotle.* London: Methuen & Co., Ltd., 1949.

Sherif, Muzafer, *An Outline of Social Psychology.* New York: Harper & Brothers, 1948.

Simon, Herbert A., *Administrative Behavior,* 2nd ed. New York: The Macmillan Co., 1955.

Smith, George Albert, and Christensen, C. Roland, *Policy Formulation and Administration,* rev. ed. Homewood: Richard D. Irwin, Inc., 1955.

Smith, Vincent E., *The Elements of Logic.* Milwaukee: The Bruce Publishing Co., 1956.

Stigler, G. J., *The Theory of Price.* New York: The Macmillan Co., 1946.

Taylor, Frederick W., *The Principles of Scientific Management.* New York: Harper & Brothers, 1911.

Tead, Ordway, *The Art of Administration*. New York: McGraw-Hill Book Co., 1951.

Terry, George R., *Principles of Management*. Homewood: Richard D. Irwin., Inc., 1953.

Throle, R. M. (ed.), Coombs C. O., and Davis, R. L., *Decision Processes*. New York: John Wiley & Sons, Inc., 1954.

Turner, William, *Lessons in Logic*. Washington, D. C.: The Catholic Education Press, 1911.

Urwick, Lyndall F., *The Pattern of Management*. Minneapolis: University of Minnesota Press, 1956.

Woodworth, Robert S., and Schlossberg, Harold, *Experimental Psychology*, rev. ed. New York: Henry Holt & Co., 1954.

ARTICLES

Bales, Robert F., "In Conference," *Harvard Business Review*, Vol. 32, No. 2 (1954), 44–50.

Bates, James, "A Model for the Science of Decision," *Philosophy of Science*, Vol. 21 (1954), 326–339.

Berwitz, C. J., "Securing Uniform Decisions in Similar Judgmental Situations," *Advanced Management*, XXII (January, 1957), 10–13.

Billings, Marion Leroy, "Problem-Solving in Different Fields of Endeavor," *The American Journal of Psychology*, XLVI, No. 2 (April, 1934), 259–272.

Blend, D. W., "Point of Decision," *Dun's Review and Modern Industry* (July, 1956), 40.

Bryson, Lyman, "Notes on Theory of Advice," *Political Science Quarterly*, LXVI, No. 3 (September, 1951), 321–339.

Bullis, Harry A., "Some Business Yardsticks," *Advanced Management*, XVI, No. 3 (March, 1951), 5–7.

Burack, Benjamin, "The Nature and Efficacy of Methods of Attack on Reasoning Problems," *Psychological Monographs*, LXIV, No. 7 (1950), 1–25.

Calhoun, S. Reed, and Green, Paul E., "Simulation: Versatile Aid to Decision-Making," *Advanced Management*, Vol. 23, No. 4 (April, 1958), 11–16.

Cartwright, D., and Festinger, L., "A Quantitative Theory of Decision," *Psychological Review*, Vol. 50 (1943), 595–621.

Corman, B. R., "The Effect of Varying Amounts and Kinds of Information as Guidance in Problem Solving," *Psychological Monographs — General and Applied*, LXXI, No. 2 (1957).

Coser, R. L., "Authority and Decision-Making in a Hospital," *American Sociological Review*, XXIII, No. 1 (February, 1958), 56–63.

Courtis, S. A., "How to Influence the Behavior of Others," *Advanced Management*, IX, No. 4 (October-December, 1944), 159–163.

Crawford, Robert W., "Operations Research and Its Role in Business Decisions," *Planning for Efficient Production*, Manufacturing Series No. 206 (AMA) (1953), 3–15.

Cyert, Richard M., Simon, Herbert A., and others, "Observation of a Business Decision," *Journal of Business*, XXIX, No. 4 (October, 1956), 237–248.

Dale, Ernest, "New Perspectives in Managerial Decision-Making," *Journal of Business*, XXVI (January, 1953), 1–8.

—— "Centralization vs. Decentralization," *Advanced Management*, XX (June, 1955), 11–16.

Danielson, L. E., and Maier, N. R. F., "Supervisory Problems in Decision-Making," *Personnel Psychology*, X, No. 2 (Summer, 1957), 169.

Dean, Joel, "Measurement of Profits for Executive Decisions," *The Accounting Review*, No. 26 (April, 1951), 185–196.

Dennison, Henry S., "Decision-Making at the Top Executive Level," *Papers and Proceedings of the Sixty-Third Annual Meeting of the American Economic Association*, Chicago, December 27 to December 30, 1950, XLI, No. 2 (AEA) (1951), 98–105.

Dewey, John, "Inquiry and Indeterminateness of Situations," *The Journal of Philosophy*, XXXIX, No. 11 (May, 1942), 290–296.

✓ Diesing, Paul, "Noneconomic Decision-Making," *Ethics*, Vol. 66 (1955), 18–35.

Dohrovolsky, S. P., "Depreciation Policies and Investment Decisions," *American Economic Review*, XLI, No. 5 (December, 1951), 906–914.

Drucker, Peter, "How to Make a Business Decision," *Nation's Business*, Vol. 44, No. 4 (April, 1956), 38, 39, 68–71.

Dubin, Robert, "Decision-Making by Management in Industrial Relations," *American Journal of Sociology*, Vol. 54 (1949), 292–297.

Duncan, O. D., and others. "Formal Devices for Making Selected Decisions," *American Journal of Sociology,* LVIII (1953), 573–585.

Durkin, Helen, "Trial and Error, Gradual Analysis and Sudden Reorganization," *Archives of Psychology,* XXX, No. 210 (May, 1937), 5–83.

Earley, James S., "Recent Developments in Cost Accounting and the Marginal Analysis," *Journal of Political Economy,* Vol. XII, No. 3 (June, 1955), 227–242.

Easton, William H., "Creative Thinking and How to Develop It," *Mechanical Engineering,* LXVIII, No. 8 (August, 1946), 697–704.

Edwards, W., "The Prediction of Decisions Among Bets," *Journal of Applied Psychology,* L (1955), 201–214.

―――― "The Theory of Decision-Making," *Psychological Bulletin,* Vol. 51 (1954), 380–417.

"Embattled Economists, The," *Forbes,* Vol. 81, No. 12 (June 15, 1958), 17–21.

Fair, E. W., "Looking Into Successful Decision-Making," *Industrial Marketing,* Vol. 42 (November, 1957), 52–53.

Flanders, Ralph E., "How Are Top Executive Decisions Made?" *Papers and Proceedings of the Sixty-Third Annual Meeting of the American Economic Association,* Chicago, December 27 to December 30, 1950, XLI, No. 2 (AEA) (1951), 93–97.

Friedman, Milton, and Savage, L. J., "The Utility Analysis of Choices Involving Risk," *Journal of Political Economy,* Vol. 56 (1948), 279–304.

Gaumnitz, R. K., and Brownlee, O. H., "Mathematics for Decision-Makers," *Harvard Business Review,* XXXIV (May, 1956), 48–56.

Girshick, M. A., "An Elementary Survey of Statistical Decision Theory," *Review of Educational Research,* XXIV (1954), 448–466.

Glover, John G., "Management Policy," *Advanced Management,* No. 18 (March, 1953), 24–27.

Golomski, W. A., "Linear Programming for Industry," *Marquette Business Review,* Vol. 1, No. 1 (June, 1957), 22–25.

Gore, W. J., "Administrative Decision-Making in Federal Field Offices," *Public Administration Review,* XVI (Autumn, 1956), 281–291.

Gros, Doctor, "Un Professeur de Reflexion pour Cadres Superieurs," *Realités-Femina Illustration* (March, 1958), 28.

Gyr, John, "Analysis of Committee Member Behavior in Four Cultures," *Human Relations,* Vol. 4 (1951), 193–202.

Hall, R. L., and Hitch, C. J., "Price Theory and Business Behaviour," *Oxford Economic Papers,* No. 2 (May, 1939), 13–45.

Hedges, Stephen B., "What Is the Right Approach to Business Problem Thinking?" *Advanced Management,* XIX, No. 3 (March, 1953), 22–24.

Henderson, Alexander, and Schlaifer, Robert, "Mathematical Programming — Better Information for Better Decision-Making," *Harvard Business Review,* Vol. 32, No. 3 (1954), 73–100.

Henry, K., "Pushbutton Decisions: How Far Ahead? (Computer as Decision-Making Tool)," *Dun's Review and Modern Industry,* Vol. 71 (February, 1958), 46–47.

——— "When Presidents Decide," *Dun's Review and Modern Industry,* Vol. 70, No. 5 (November, 1957), 33–35, 51–64.

Herrold, K. F., and others, "Difficulties Encountered in Group Decision-Making," *Personnel and Guidance Journal,* Vol. 31 (May, 1953), 516–523.

Hunt, L. I., "Decisions and Their Significance," *The Management Review,* XXXI, No. 10 (October, 1942), 329, 332–333.

Hurni, M. L., "Decision-Making in the Age of Automation," *Harvard Business Review,* XXXIII, No. 5 (September, 1955), 49–58.

Hurwicz, Leonid, "Game Theory and Decisions," *Scientific American,* Vol. 192, No. 2 (February, 1955), 78–83.

Husband, Richard Wellington, "Cooperative Versus Solitary Problem Solution," *The Journal of Social Psychology,* XI, Second Half (May, 1940), 405–409.

Hutchins, Robert M., "The Task of the Administrator is Ordering the Means to an End," *Modern Hospital,* No. 71 (November, 1948), 51–54.

"Industrial Diagnostics: A Systematic Approach to Management-Problem Solving," *The Management Review,* XLVI (June, 1957), 79.

Ingham, Samuel D., "Physiology of Thinking," *Bulletin of the Los Angeles Neurological Society,* VIII, No. 3 (September, 1943), 69–74.

Irwin, F. W., and Smith, W. A. S., "Value, Cost and Information

BIBLIOGRAPHY   193

as Determinants of Decision," *Journal of Experimental Psychology,* LIV, No. 3 (September, 1957), 229–232.

Jarchow, Christian E., "The Influence of Reports on Top Management Decisions," *The Controller,* No. 19 (May, 1951), 206–208, 210–212, 222–223.

Johnson, Donald M., "A Modern Account of Problem-Solving," *The Psychological Bulletin,* XLI, No. 4 (April, 1944), 201–229.
——— "Problem Solving and Symbolic Processes," *Annual Review of Psychology,* (1950), 297–310.

Jones, Thomas Roy, "Proper Decisions Mark the Successful Man of Business," *The Inland Printer,* CXIII, No. 6 (September, 1944), 51.

Kahn, Robert L., and Connell, Charles F., "Nobody Tells Me Anything! Getting the Facts You Need for Decision," *Dun's Review and Modern Industry,* Vol. 70, No. 5 (November, 1957), 36–38, 98–107.

Kamm, J. O., "Making Business Decisions," *Advanced Management,* XVI, No. 2 (February, 1951), 10–13.

Katona, George, "Psychological Analysis of Business Decisions and Expectations," *The American Economic Review,* XXXVI, No. 1 (March, 1946), 44–62.

Katona, George, and Morgan, J. N., "The Quantitative Study of Factors Determining Business Decisions," *Quarterly Journal of Economics,* LXVI, No. 1 (February, 1952), 67–90.

Kerlinger, Fred N., "Decision-Making in Japan," *Social Forces,* XXX, No. 1 (October, 1951), 36–41.

Kimball, George E., "Decision Theory: Operations Research in Management," *Advanced Management,* XIX, No. 12 (December, 1954), 5–7.

Kubly, Harold E., "Are Your Decisions Reflective or Intuitive?" *Advanced Management,* XVIII, No. 6 (June, 1953), 5–7.

"Learning Can Be Fun, Even for Busy Executives, AMA's Decision-Making Game," *Business Week* (May 4, 1957), 164.

Lefford, Arthur, "The Influence of Emotional Subject Matter on Logical Reasoning," *Journal of General Psychology,* XXXIV, Second Half (April, 1946), 127–151.

"Light on Deciding — Carnegie Studies on Decision-Making," *Business Week* (April 13, 1957), 184.

Lipson, Harry A., "Decision Making in Smaller Stores," *Journal of Retailing,* XXVIII, No. 1 (Spring, 1952), 23–27, 46.

Lunbrew, H. E., "Policy Determination," *Advanced Management,* Vol. 22, No. 9 (September, 1957), 6.

McCamy, James L., "Analysis of the Process of Decision-Making," *Public Administration Review,* VII, No. 1 (Winter, 1947), 41–48.

McDonald, John, "How Businessmen Make Decisions," *Fortune,* LII, No. 2 (August, 1955), 84–87, 130, 132, 137.

McDonald, John, and Ricciardi, Frank, "The Business Decision Game," *Fortune,* LVII, No. 3 (March, 1958), 140–142, 208.

Maffei, R. B., "Mathematical Models, Values of Parameters, and the Sensitivity Analysis of Management — Decision Rules," *Journal of Marketing,* XXI (April, 1957), 419.

Maier, Norman R. F., "The Quality of Group Decisions as Influenced by the Discussion Leader," *Human Relations,* Vol. 3 (1950), 155–174.

—— "An Aspect of Human Reasoning," *The British Journal of Psychology,* XXIV, Part 2 (October, 1933), 144–155.

—— "Reasoning in Humans: I. On Directions," *The Journal of Comparative Psychology,* X, No. 2 (April, 1930), 115–143.

—— "Reasoning in Humans: II. The Solution of a Problem and Its Appearance in Consciousness," *The Journal of Comparative Psychology,* XII, No. 2 (August, 1931), 181–194.

—— "Reasoning in Humans: III. The Mechanisms of Equivalent Stimuli and of Reasoning," *Journal of Experimental Psychology,* XXXV, No. 4, (August, 1945), 349–360.

—— "The Behavior Mechanisms Concerned with Problem "Solving," *Psychological Review,* XLVII, No. 1 (January, 1940), 43–58.

Malinowski, Bronislaw, "Culture as a Determinant of Behavior," *The Scientific Monthly,* XLIII (November, 1936), 440–449.

Marquart, D. I., "Group Problem Solving," *Journal of Social Psychology,* Vol. 41 (1955), pp. 103–113.

Marschak, Jacob, "Rational Behavior, Uncertain Prospects and Measurable Utility," *Econometrica,* XVIII, No. 2 (April, 1950), 111–141.

Martin, N. H., "Differential Decisions in the Management of an Industrial Plant," *Journal of Business,* XXIX, No. 4 (October, 1956), 249–260.

Miller, W. Wesley, "Costs for Plans and Policies," *National Association of Cost Accountants Bulletin,* No. 29 (September 15, 1947), 55–64.

Mills, E. S., "The Theory of Inventory Decisions," *Econometrica*, XXV, No. 2 (April, 1957), 222.

Morell, R. W., "Managerial Decision-Making — A Challenge," *Marquette Business Review*, I, No. 3 (December, 1957), 1–6.

—— "Analysis of Stages in Decision-Making," *Research Bulletin No. 106*, University of Detroit Press (January, 1958), 1–12.

—— "What is a Decision?" *Hospital Progress*, Vol. 39, No. 2 (February, 1958), 74, 95.

—— "Operations Research in Decision-Making," *Marquette Business Review*, II, No. 5 (December, 1950), 22.

Morgan, John J., and Morton, James T., "The Distortion of Syllogistic Reasoning Produced by Personal Convictions," *The Journal of Social Psychology*, XX, First Half (August, 1944), 39–59.

Muther, R., "Techniques for Making Better Decisions," *Management Review*, VL (October, 1956), 821.

Oppenheim, Felix E., "Rational Choice," *Journal of Philosophy*, Vol. 50, No. 12 (1953), 341–350.

Reiter, S., "Surrogates for Uncertain Decision Problems; Minimal Information for Decision-Making," *Econometrica*, XXV, No. 2 (April, 1957), 339–345.

Ricciardi, F. M., "Business War Games for Executives, AMA's Top Management Decision Game," *Management Review*, XXXXVI (May, 1957), 45.

Robinson, James A., "Decision-Making in the House Rules Committee," *Administrative Science Quarterly*, III, No. 1 (June, 1958), 73–86.

Robinson, W. S., "The Logical Structure of Analytic Induction," *American Sociological Review*, XVI, No. 6 (December, 1951), 812–818.

Rossi, Peter H., "Community Decision-Making," *Administrative Science Quarterly*, Vol. 1, No. 4 (March, 1957), 415–443.

Shock, Nathan, W., "Some Psychophysiological Relations," *The Psychological Bulletin*, XXXVI, No. 6 (June, 1939), 447–476.

Shubik, Martin, "The Uses of Game Theory in Management Science," *Management Science*, Vol. 2 (1955), 40–54.

Siefkin, Forest D., "Executive Decisions at the Top Level," *Papers and Proceedings of the Sixty-Third Annual Meeting of the American Economic Association*, Chicago, December 27 to December 30, 1950, XLI, No. 2 (AEA) (1951), 88–92.

Siegel, S., "Levels of Aspiration and Decision-Making," *Psychological Review*, LXIV, No. 4 (July, 1957), 253–262.

Simon, Herbert A., "Decision-Making and Administrative Organization," *Public Administration Review*, IV, No. 1 (Winter, 1944), 16–30.

Smith, N. M., and others, "The Theory of Value and the Science of Decision, A Summary," *Journal of the Operations Research Society of America*, I (1953), 103–113.

Smithe, Mason, "Presenting the Facts for Disciplined Business Decisions," *National Association of Cost Accountants Bulletin*, XXIX, No. 24 (August, 1948), 1523–1532.

Solow, Herbert, "Operations Research Is in Business," *Fortune*, Vol. 53 (February, 1956), 128–131.

Symonds, Gifford, H., "Mathematical Programming as an Aid to Decision-Making," *Advanced Management*, Vol. XX, No. 5 (May, 1955), 11–17.

Talacko, J., "Linear Programming as a Tool of the Business Executive," *Marquette Business Review*, Vol. 1, No. 3 (December, 1957), 23–29.

Tannenbaum, Robert, "Managerial Decision-Making," *The Journal of Business*, XXIII, No. 1 (January, 1950), 22–39.

Tannenbaum, Robert, and Massarick, Fred, "Participation by Subordinates in the Managerial Decision-Making Process," *Canadian Journal of Economics and Political Science*, XVI (August, 1950), 408–418.

Taylor, Donald W., and McNemar, Olga W., "Problem Solving and Thinking," *Annual Review of Psychology*, Vol. 6 (1955), 455–482.

"Ten Top Executives, How They Make Decisions," *Factory Management*, CXIII, No. 1 (January, 1955), 140–144.

Toohey, J. J., "Propositions, Judgment, and Inference," *The Journal of Philosophy*, XXXVII, No. 9 (April, 1940), 232–243.

Watson, Alfred N., "Operations Research and Financial Planning," *Techniques and Data for Planning Financial Policy*, Financial Management Series No. 102 (AMA) (1952), 3–12.

Weimer, Arthur M., "Business and General Education," *Indiana Business Review*, Vol. 32, No. 6 (June, 1957), 5–11.

"What's Ahead for Operations Research," *Business Week* (August 27, 1955), 65.

Woodworth, Robert S., and Sells, Saul B., "An Atmosphere Effect in Formal Syllogistic Reasoning," *Journal of Experimental Psychology*, XVIII, No. 4 (August, 1935), 451–460.

INDEX